Nordic Film Classics
METTE HJORT AND PETER SCHEPELERN, *Series Editors*

NORDIC FILM CLASSICS

The Nordic Film Classics series offers in-depth studies of key films by Danish, Finnish, Icelandic, Norwegian, and Swedish directors. Written by emerging as well as established film scholars, and where possible in conversation with relevant film practitioners, these books help to shed light on the ways in which the Nordic nations and region have contributed to the art of film.

Ingmar Bergman's The Silence: *Pictures in the Typewriter, Writings on the Screen* by Maaret Koskinen

Dagur Kári's Nói the Albino by Björn Norðfjörð

Lone Scherfig's Italian for Beginners by Mette Hjort

Lukas Moodysson's Show Me Love by Anna Westerståhl Stenport

Thomas Vinterberg's Festen *(The Celebration)* by C. Claire Thomson

Thomas Vinterberg's
Festen
(THE CELEBRATION)

C. Claire Thomson

UNIVERSITY OF WASHINGTON PRESS
Seattle

MUSEUM TUSCULANUM PRESS
Copenhagen

THIS BOOK IS MADE POSSIBLE BY A COLLABORATIVE GRANT FROM
THE ANDREW W. MELLON FOUNDATION.

Publication of this book is supported by a generous grant from the Scan/Design Foundation.

© 2013 by the University of Washington Press

18 17 16 15 14 13   5 4 3 2 1

All rights reserved. No part of this publication may be reproduced or transmitted in any form or by any means, electronic or mechanical, including photocopy, recording, or any information storage or retrieval system, without permission in writing from the publisher.

Published in the United States by
UNIVERSITY OF WASHINGTON PRESS
PO Box 50096, Seattle, WA 98145, USA
www.washington.edu/uwpress

Published in Europe by
MUSEUM TUSCULANUM PRESS
University of Copenhagen
Birketinget 6, DK-2300 Copenhagen S, Denmark
www.mtp.dk
978 87 635 4113 8

LIBRARY OF CONGRESS CATALOGING-IN-PUBLICATION DATA

Thomson, C. Claire.
Thomas Vinterberg's Festen (The celebration) / C. Claire Thomson.
   pages cm. — (Nordic film classics)
Includes bibliographical references.
ISBN 978-0-295-99298-3 (pbk.)
1. Festen (Motion picture). I. Title.
PN1997.F418T57 2013
791.43'72—dc23   2013015088

The paper used in this publication is acid-free and meets the minimum requirements of American National Standard for Information Sciences—Permanence of Paper for Printed Library Materials, ANSI Z39.48–1984.∞

For Lizzi, my hero

Contents

Acknowledgments	ix
Introduction	3

PART I. *FESTEN* AND FILM HISTORY

1	*Dogma 95 and Danish Cinema*	17
2	*The Auteur and Cinema History*	37
3	*Dogma 95 and the Death of Film*	51

PART II. *FESTEN*'S BODIES

4	*The Handheld Camera*	73
5	*The Hotel*	91
6	*Sense Memory and the Haptic*	108

PART III. *FESTEN*'S GHOSTS

7 *The Story of Allan*   127
8 Festen *from Screen to Stage*   139
9 *Media and Time*   151

Appendix A. Dogma 95 Manifesto and Vow of Chastity   163
Appendix B. *Festen*: Data   167
Appendix C. Thomas Vinterberg: An Annotated Filmography   171
Notes   179
Bibliography   201
Index   213

Acknowledgments

I have had countless conversations about *Festen* with many, many individuals over the years, in academic, public, and recreational contexts. The richest and most challenging discussions have taken place in the classroom, and I owe an enormous vote of thanks to the very many enthusiastic and talented B.A., M.A., and Ph.D. students of Nordic Cinema at the University of East Anglia (UEA), Norwich (2000–2004); University College London (UCL) (2005–2012); Åbo Akademi, Finland (2008); and Vilnius University, Lithuania (2011). I am all too aware that much of what I have written in this book probably originated in thoughts shared in a seminar or essay.

Mette Hjort and Peter Schepelern, series editors of Nordic Film Classics, and Jacquie Ettinger, Tim Zimmermann, and Mary C. Ribesky at University of Washington Press, as well as Tim Roberts of the Modern Language Initiative, have all been patient and sympathetic well beyond the call of duty while successive unexpected administrative obligations at UCL ate into my research and writing time and delayed completion of the manuscript. I am very grateful indeed to them for granting me the extra time required and for all their help and support. I would also like to thank Jane M. Lichty for careful and thoughtful editing of the manuscript.

Warm thanks are also due to Bodil Marie Stavning Thomsen for her invaluable comments on the manuscript, to Geraldine Brodie for sharing her insights into *Festen* onstage, to Andrew Nestingen, who did much to shape the initial book proposal, and to an anonymous peer reviewer for thought-provoking criticisms. Diane Negra's enthusiasm for the project convinced me that *Festen* was a film worth fighting for. Anne Mette Traberg Jørgensen, my former M.A. student, very kindly shared her interview with Thomas Vinterberg with me, and Thomas Vinterberg generously allowed use of the resulting material. Lisbeth Richter Larsen and other staff at the Danish Film Institute have been unfailingly helpful.

On a more personal note, I would like to extend special thanks to Jakob Stougaard-Nielsen, Mary Hilson, Elettra Carbone, and especially Carol O'Sullivan, who have been steadfast sources of encouragement, lively conversation, and inspirational scholarship over the years. Steve Cross has asked usefully (im)pertinent questions about film studies and its wider social relevance, challenging me to think in new ways about scholarship and media practice. Karin Charles has been the calm rock at the heart of our department, enabling me to carve out time to write. My parents, Robert and Catherine Thomson, and my sister, Lizzi Thomson, have provided thought-provoking feedback as well as moral support.

Finally, grateful thanks are due to the Scan|Design Foundation, which very generously supported publication of this volume.

Thomas Vinterberg's *Festen* (The Celebration)

Introduction

In late March 1995, the Danish director Lars von Trier stood on a podium in the Théâtre de l'Odéon in Paris. He was clad in a lumberjack shirt and laden with plastic bags. Below him, the audience, resplendent in tuxedos and gowns, had assembled to mark the centenary of cinema. Von Trier's contribution to the party was printed on the red leaflets stuffed into his plastic bags. When his moment came, he read the text aloud: the Dogma 95 manifesto and Vow of Chastity. He scattered the red papers over the heads of the crowd below, declined to take questions, and left.[1]

Undersigned by von Trier and Thomas Vinterberg, the Dogma 95 manifesto declared itself a "rescue action." The cinema had become corrupted by "the film of illusion" and "the individual film." The Vow of Chastity proposed ten commandments that would strip props, sets, genre, special effects, postproduction tweaks, and aesthetic strategies out of the filmmaking process. The Vow would provide a creative fillip for the director—but the director would not be credited.

Von Trier's intervention in the centenary celebrations was dismissed as a stunt by some critics and journalists, while others waited expectantly for the progeny that would be spawned by this new Dogma.² Their patience would be tested. While the year of its launch lingered on in the name of the movement, the first two films made under the auspices of Dogma 95 would not premiere until spring 1998. The reasons behind this delay are primarily prosaic: the cultural politics of film finance. But this three-year window of time coincided with one of those extended moments in film history where institutional and technological change become manifestly and inextricably entangled with shifts in practices of production, distribution, and consumption.

This book is all about the first film to premiere under the Dogma 95 banner in 1998: *Festen* (The Celebration), often referred to as *Dogme #1: Festen*, and directed by an uncredited Vinterberg.³ To devote such a degree of attention to one film is an expression of the profound and complex viewing pleasure that one film can inspire and the multiplicity of readings that a rich film text can sustain. But *Festen* warrants close examination for other reasons: it constitutes a rich and complex case study in how the technological, cultural, and film-historical developments just mentioned meet and merge around the period from 1995 to 1998.

It is not hard to find anecdotal and statistical evidence of the mark *Festen* has made on the critical and popular imagination in both the Danish and global film contexts. From the outset, it broke records: by summer 1998, an estimated one million Danes (about a fifth of the population) had seen the film in the cinema and/or on television.⁴ Iconic directors declared themselves enamored of the film: Ingmar Bergman described *Festen* as "one of the best films I've seen," while Nicolas Cage inquired about buying the rights to a U.S. remake.⁵ Vinterberg was deluged with invitations to make feature films and pop videos.

However, while quantitative measures such as box office sales and viewing figures shed some light on the impact of a film in the short term, a more complex symbiosis of factors must be taken into account in order to grasp its significance for film history. We cannot understand the impact or the import of *Festen* without considering its cultural context: the state of Danish cinema in the 1990s, the film-historical narratives into which the Dogma 95 manifesto inscribes itself, and, not least, the productive symbiosis of constraint and creativity engendered by the Vow of Chastity. Equally, we might claim that we can come to a more nuanced understanding of that same cultural and technological context by engaging closely with key films of the time, such as *Festen*.

I use the biological metaphor "symbiosis" advisedly, for it implies two things. First, "symbiosis" implies mutual dependency among different actors;[6] we cannot always separate out cause and effect. For example, in terms of its conception, its realization, and its reception, *Festen* cannot be considered independently of Dogma 95. The movement and its regulations shaped *Festen* as a text, but *Festen* was the first film to translate those rules into practice, thus transforming Dogma 95 from an untested whimsy to a protean source of creativity. What is more, the trajectory of the story that inspired *Festen*—from the imagination of a troubled young man to radio program, to film script, to screen, and to stage—is fascinating in and of itself and has much to tell us about how memes travel between media and how form begets content (see chapter 7). This book is intended to flesh out at least the most essential aspects of the cultural and critical environment into which *Festen* was born and to pay special attention to certain chapters in the story of *Festen* (such as the saga of the radio interview that inspired the screenplay) that are less well known to a non-Danish audience.

The second implication of "symbiosis" is the adaptive collaboration of different actors in response to particular environmental circumstances or challenges. For example, *Festen* was shot on digital video due to cost constraints engendered by the experimental nature of the project, and this decision had implications for the film's style, for its critical reception, for Vinterberg's career, and, arguably, for cinema history. But all these effects must be understood in the technological and film-cultural context that obtained around the millennium: What kind of digital cameras and editing facilities were available? What kinds of cultural ideas about the digital were in circulation, and how were these inflected by *Festen* and other digitally shot Dogma 95 films? As we shall see, *Festen* and Dogma 95 could not have emerged as they did in another period of film history; they were shaped by, and contributed to shaping, late-twentieth-century developments in film aesthetics, politics, and technology. To pay such a degree of attention to one film is, then, necessarily to stake a claim to its significance for film history. It is an investment in the potential of one film to encapsulate or embody many of the key film-historical, aesthetic, and technological debates and developments of its era. A dozen years on, *Dogme #1: Festen* can be seen as a film that not only acted as a lightning rod for ongoing changes in Danish film culture but also constituted a key text in the transition between analogue and digital cinema on an international scale.

Is the hindsight of a decade or so sufficient to begin to grasp the long-term ramifications of Dogma 95 and its first film? In the case of *Festen* and other influential productions made just before the turn of the millennium, we have to contend with the notorious rearview mirror effect, according to which recent artifacts or texts loom larger on the highway of history. *Festen* featured, for example, in the select list of ten films granted a place in the Danish Cultural Canon of 2006.[7] We know that *Festen* will at least prevail as a footnote in future histories of cinema as the vanguard of digital video filmmaking. But what of it? Will what we call new media today define the moving image in the twenty-first century just as film defined the twentieth, or will the cinema historiographers of the future trace quite a different narrative, a narrative in which, perhaps, technologies from around the millennium might be a developmental dead end?[8]

We cannot, of course, second-guess the verdict of future film historians on *Festen* and other films from the turn of the millennium. What we can already observe, though, is that film theory and film philosophy have moved on since 1998, in large part by dint of the new technologies that emerged around that time. It is my contention that *Festen* warrants and deserves more sustained and nuanced analysis than it has hitherto been accorded—on its own terms, as a film text, and in light of recent critical-theoretical work in film and visual culture. On one level, this is an intellectual endeavor; on another level, it is also deeply personal and subjective. To make an argument for my chosen approach to *Festen*, I have to start by remembering my affective response to it.

Sometime in 1999, at the Filmhouse cinema in Edinburgh, Scotland, I saw *Festen* for the first time. I don't remember feeling seasick, as some of my friends reported after their first experience of a film shot on a handheld camera and projected on the big screen. I do remember feeling, as the lights went up afterward, a profound joy that such a film existed. I felt *touched* by this film, more than I ever had before or since upon first encountering a new movie. In the years in between, I have taught and written on emerging theories of cinematic affect and texture and felt increasingly compelled to try to get to the bottom of why *Festen*—the harbinger of a new generation of feature films to register the material world in the form of digital code—should feel so tangible.

While I was feeling around for answers, the film got lost. *Festen* got lost in the searchlights of a thousand interviews with a suddenly famous, exhausted, endlessly articulate, and generously forthcoming director. *Festen* got lost in a welter of criticism and discussion of

Dogma 95, the manifesto that spawned it. *Festen* got lost, in Denmark, in a long-running press controversy about the legitimacy of the story that inspired it. *Festen* got lost in the tendency of film critics the world over to petrify it as the defining moment of a directorial career that had barely begun. And *Festen* got lost in the compelling, seductive power of its own story, a story so beautifully structured and so translatable across media that it has metamorphosed, to almost unanimous praise, into stage adaptations across the European continent, in London's West End, and on Broadway. This book has become an exercise in finding the film again, an exercise in letting the film touch me again, and perhaps you, and trying to explain how it does so.

It is for this reason that I have deliberately shied away from structuring this book around empirical research, at least to the same extent that other books in the Nordic Film Classics series have successfully done. I think that *Festen* is already amply served by (quite literally) hundreds of interviews, reviews, documentaries, and similar treatments published in English and other languages and readily available to a wide audience. Many of the most comprehensive essays and interviews are listed in the bibliography. *Purity and Provocation*, a 2003 anthology edited by Mette Hjort and Scott MacKenzie, did much to fill the gaps in "fully blown scholarly analysis" of the Dogma phenomenon that were apparent at the time.[9] Yet even that first-rate volume lacks a sustained, critical-theoretically inflected aesthetic analysis of *Festen*. This is not to say that the copious empirical materials and extant scholarship available are not invaluable; I have made extensive use of published interviews and reviews, as well as a lengthy interview that Vinterberg kindly granted to my former M.A. student Anne Mette Traberg Jørgensen. However, on the whole, my instinct has been to try to let the film breathe, to release the film as a text from the weight of extant interpretations and explanations, to reinvest it with sensuality.

One means of doing so has been to linger on the multisensory appeal of *Festen* as audiovisual text. Analyses of *Festen* that engage closely with how the film *looks* are rare.[10] Is this because of the invocation in the Dogma 95 manifesto that the director should refrain from aesthetic judgment and personal taste? We have no reason to doubt Vinterberg's word that he really did consciously avoid making aesthetically motivated decisions while shooting *Festen*. That doesn't mean there is no "style" or texture to analyze, as Vinterberg himself insisted in an interview in 2000: "I experienced real irritation at not being able to cultivate a visual aesthetic because the Dogme rules literally prohibit that. Secondly, it turned out that in following the rules we were generating something that resembled an aesthetic in its own right, and as a result I virtually didn't have to think about that aspect of the film."[11]

The manifesto's ban on "aesthetic judgment" and "personal taste" might at first glance seem to free us from the ghost that usually haunts textual interpretation: intentionality. As the above quotation suggests, however, the refusal to adopt an overarching aesthetic strategy is replaced in Dogma 95 by another kind of intentionality: an amalgam of agents and actants engaged in well-documented, on-the-spot problem solving in response to the Dogma 95 rules.[12] Nevertheless, while acknowledging Vinterberg's prodigious talent as a director and the many and varied ingenious reactions of the cast and crew in their responses to Dogma 95 strictures, this book is first and foremost about the film, not the filmmakers.

Another concept fundamental to my approach to *Festen* is "affect." The concept requires commentary here. In this book, "affect" refers to a dimension of the spectator's response to a film image that is preconscious and that implicates both body and mind. *Affect* is not a synonym for *emotion*. Brian Massumi has shown how embodied response to images operates at (at least) two levels. One level involves physical responses (e.g., a racing heart) to the content (e.g., the narrative) of a visual stimulus; the other level seems to have little to do with content and more to do with what he calls "intensity," a concept we still barely have the vocabulary to describe or measure.[13] Barbara M. Kennedy expresses very well how affective response is entangled with a broader spectrum of experience in the encounter with cinema: "The cinematic experience is more than just the scopic or the visual. The aesthetics of the experiential are encompassed across the synaesthetic, the kinaesthetic, the proprioceptive and the processuality of duration and movement. The aesthetic then in this sense might be perceived as part of a material emotion, felt at a level deeper than a psychically constructed subjectivity."[14]

Incorporating a consideration of affect into our analyses of cultural texts is an essential project for our time, thinks Massumi: "There seems to be a growing feeling within media, literary, and art theory that affect is central to an understanding of our information- and image-based late capitalist culture, in which so-called master narratives are perceived to have foundered."[15] More recently, in a similar vein, Steven Shaviro has argued for the importance of studying new media productions as "affective maps" and coproducers of the "social relations, flows, and feelings" they tackle.[16] Attempting to grasp what kinds of affects might be triggered by *Festen*, the first digitally shot feature film, is a crucial dimension of our appreciation of how it impacts the viewer and maps the cultural context from which it emerged.

The book is organized into three sections, each containing three chapters. Part 1, "*Festen* and Film History," situates *Festen* at the intersection of three historical narratives, each of which reaches some kind of turning point in the period from 1995 to 1998. The first of these is Danish cinema history. Chapter 1 outlines the origins of Dogma 95 and contextualizes these within developments in Danish film and culture. Chapter 2 takes up the Dogma 95 manifesto's challenge to the French New Wave and other key moments in cinema history. In exploring Dogma 95's stance on "the individual film," we discuss the concept of the auteur and how the associated discourses have impinged on Vinterberg's directorial career. Chapter 3 considers another historiographical narrative that emerged in the wake of the millennium and the advent of the digital: the so-called "end" or "death" of film. The concepts that have been developed by scholars over the past decade in an effort to come to terms with seismic changes in the medium are essential to our understanding of the cultural import of *Festen* and also to our appreciation of its material instantiation.

Part 2 focuses on *Festen*'s bodies. In chapter 4, we follow the body of the camera operator as he or she in turn follows the actors, exploring the possibilities of the handheld digital video camera, and we try to trace the influence of earlier experiments in handheld filmmaking. Chapter 5 maps the movement of bodies in space and time through the film's location, the hotel. Chapter 6 examines the appropriation of objects (props and sets) in the hotel and the role of sense memory and haptic texturality in the film. These chapters suggest that from the Dogma 95 rules emerge post-indexical guarantees of the integrity of the pro-filmic environment. Put differently, the pragmatic decision to shoot *Festen* on digital video robs the viewer of the traditional certainty that the film offers "unmodified photographic recordings of real events that took place in real, physical space."[17] Nevertheless, the handheld digital video camera facilitates relationships between body, space, image, and viewer that work to produce "reality effects" and seduce the viewer into an "affective contract" with the text, a dynamic that Danish media scholars Britta Timm Knudsen and Bodil Marie Thomsen see as typical of the media landscape of the time.[18]

By all accounts, *Festen* was intended to be more of a supernatural story than it turned out to be. Part 3 resurrects some of the ghostly presences that flit around the film. The first of these, in chapter 7, is the story of Allan, the radio interviewee who inspired Vinterberg to write the treatment for *Festen* but whose story turned out to be a complex fabrication. Chapter 8 discusses another set of intertexts—the versions of *Festen* rewritten for the stage—and their reworkings of space, style, and story for the theater. Chapter 9 functions to draw the book's red threads together, recapitulating *Festen*'s status as digital object, returning not just to the ghost of the dead sister but also to the ghosts of Danish cinema history.

Before turning to an account of *Festen*'s genesis within the Dogma 95 movement, I offer a brief summary of the story line of *Festen*.

The film opens with the sound of a cell phone: Christian Klingenfeldt-Hansen is walking along a road somewhere in rural Denmark, on his way to the sixtieth birthday celebration for his father, Helge, a hotelier. Christian is visiting from Paris, where he is a successful restaurateur. Christian's brother, Michael, drives past and stops to let Christian into his car, obliging his wife and three children to walk the rest of the way to the hotel. It transpires that the family has not been reunited since the funeral, some months earlier, of Christian's twin sister, Linda; Michael did not attend the funeral and is less than welcome at his father's birthday. The remaining sister, Helene, descends upon the house. After a stilted confrontation with his father, Christian joins his siblings to greet the arriving guests.

While stripping dust sheets from the furniture in her late sister's room, with the help of the receptionist, Lars, Helene follows clues left on the bathroom walls and finds a letter, which clearly upsets her. Meanwhile, relationships between the main characters are mapped out in the hotel rooms, drinks are imbibed in the garden, and at six o'clock the guests convene for speeches and aperitifs, presided over by the luckless German toastmaster Helmut von Sachs.

By seven o'clock, they are at table, and the elder son, Christian, stands to make a speech. It is a revelation, a home truth speech. He recounts how his father used to sexually abuse him and his late twin sister and that he holds his father responsible for her death. The guests have no idea how to react. Christian tries to leave, but finds succor with his childhood friends, who now work in the kitchen, and resolves to continue to try to make his father face up to his crimes. Under the direction of the chef, Kim, the staff helps by hiding the guests' car keys, thus trapping the partygoers as unwilling witnesses to Christian's revelation. Christian is publicly denounced by his sister and his mother, Else, privately intimidated by his father, forcibly ejected several times, and eventually beaten by his brother and left tied to a tree in the forest.

Meanwhile, the party descends into drunkenness. Waitress Michelle repeatedly tries to confront Michael with the consequences of their drunken fling at a previous party and is beaten for her trouble. Helene's American boyfriend, Gbatokai, arrives (driven by Vinterberg in a cameo role as taxi driver) to a hostile reception from Michael and is serenaded with racist popular songs by the assembled guests. Helene develops a blinding headache and is aided by waitress Pia, who accidentally finds the letter that Helene had hidden in her tube of painkillers.

Christian escapes from the woods and returns to the house in time to hand the letter to Helene as she dances through the mansion in a conga line. After some prompting, she reads it aloud, thus corroborating her father's guilt in her dead sister's own words. The parents leave the party, devastated; Christian collapses. A dream sequence visualizes his affectionate reunion with his deceased twin, but he is summoned back to consciousness by a phone ringing and finds himself in bed with Pia. The younger guests are continuing the party downstairs, but Michael has gone missing. He is found meting out punishment to his prostrate father and is stopped by Christian just as he unzips his fly to avenge the abuse done to his siblings.

The film ends with a final scene around the breakfast table the next morning. The siblings reconcile, and Helge apologizes to his family for his wrongs. Michael asks him to leave; the mother decides to stay at the table. Christian asks Pia to come and live with him in Paris. The film concludes with a lingering shot of Christian's inscrutable face.

PART ONE

Festen and Film History

1
Dogma 95 and Danish Cinema

In September 2005, the leading British film critic, Philip French, declared in the Sunday newspaper the *Observer*: "At the moment, Denmark is producing the most thoughtful and interesting films not only in Scandinavia but in western Europe."[1] French was looking back at the extraordinary renaissance of Danish cinema since Lars von Trier's intervention in Paris a decade earlier. Other critics conducting similar retrospectives around the same time were equally complimentary: David Bordwell, for example, judged that Danish film was exceptionally successful in showing "creative vibrancy" in the spheres of mass-consumption genre films, prestige cinema, and avant-garde film and that its success could be credited in part to its "strong sense of narrative desire."[2] Mette Hjort has given us the term "New Danish Cinema" as a cooler-headed alternative to the epithet of a "new golden age" for film in Denmark, dating roughly from the late 1980s.[3] Hjort demonstrates how the conditions of possibility for New Danish Cinema began to unfurl during the decade *before* 1995. It is striking, nonetheless, that many of the key developments in the renaissance of Danish cinema—including the premiere of *Festen*—take place in or around 1998. We must, then, observe

ginning that *Festen*'s role in reinvigorating the Danish
and the status of Danish cinema worldwide can best be
understood not as cause, or as symptom, but as a productive symbiosis of circumstance.

The Transformation of the Danish Cinema Industry

To appreciate the significance of the growth in the prestige of Danish film from the late 1980s on, and the role that *Festen* played in it, we need to outline how Danish preeminence in cinema had ebbed and flowed during the twentieth century.

Denmark's first "golden age" produced some of the treasures of early and silent cinema. For a decade after the birth of cinema, Danish film production was dominated by one man, the entrepreneur and photographer Peter Elfelt, who specialized in *actualités*, especially featuring the royal family. In 1906, the founding of the Nordisk Film company by Ole Olsen marked the start of that first "golden" decade of extraordinary creativity and productivity in Danish film. During the 1910s, Nordisk Film made Denmark a leading film nation; directors such as August Blom, Holger-Madsen, and Benjamin Christensen exported spectacular productions all over the world. Asta Nielsen, or "Die Asta," emerged from Denmark as the world's first woman film star, although her career unfolded largely in Germany, while Olsen, Nordisk Film's CEO, pontificated on the role of cinema as a disseminator of cultural values.[4] By 1920, however, the Danish studios were eclipsed as a preeminent source of films that would sate popular tastes, and with the coming of sound film (and thus the end of the inherent translatability of intertitles) from the late 1920s, Danish actors and writers had to contend with the relative obscurity of their native language. Danish cinema continued to produce examples of outstanding native talent—director Carl Th. Dreyer enjoyed a half century of no little international and critical renown from 1918 to 1964—and state support kept, notably, documentaries, educational films, children's films, and popular cinema buoyant. However, by the 1980s, the industry was considered domestically to be somewhat sclerotic, and Danish film went largely unregarded on the international scene.[5]

Danish cinema needed a dramatic change of fortune. And in a twist of fate worthy of one of Hans Christian Andersen's fairytales, the late 1980s brought a little bit of magic. Danish directors won Oscars for best foreign film two years running: Gabriel Axel in 1988 for *Babettes gæstebud* (Babette's Feast) and Bille August in 1989 for *Pelle Erobreren* (Pelle the Conqueror). Mette Hjort describes the transformative effect of these Oscars on Danish cinema as "the kind of statistically unimaginable and thus quasi-prophetic event that could truly galvanize an entire milieu and make it an irresistible magnet for new talent."[6] While these two Oscar-winning films were traditional fare—costume dramas and literary adaptations to boot—von Trier was also emerging, in that same period, as a key filmmaker. His feature-film debut *The Element of Crime* had won the Prix Technique at Cannes in 1984, heralding the beginning of the sea change von Trier would unleash in Danish cinema. That von Trier's film was in English galvanized the debate in Denmark on the definition of a "Danish" film worthy of state support. A new film act in 1989 decoupled the use of the Danish language and Danish actors from the definition of a film as "Danish" and also reduced the power of the academic "consultants" who had controlled filmmakers' access to state funds.[7] In the wake of these developments, Hjort also discusses in detail the reemergence of a "popular cinephilia" in Denmark and a new generation of passionate, creative filmmaking talent, professionally educated at the well-run national Film School and carefully nurtured by a set of institutions that were reconfigured in the late 1990s.[8]

Two key developments coincided with the filming and launch of *Festen*. The Danish government enacted another new film act in 1997, merging three existing institutions under one roof: the Danish Film Institute, the Film Museum, and the National Film Board. Hjort gives an account of the objectives and the impact of the revamped Danish Film Institute. Its strategic priorities, briefly summarized, were as follows: to preserve national film heritage, to promote film culture and an inclusive cinephilia at home, to consolidate and improve the breadth and quality of Danish film production, and to promote Danish film abroad as a cinema characterized by artistic merit, a spirit of innovation, and high production values.[9]

The journey of Dogma 95 from concept to body of films spans this crucial period of institutional reconfiguration and can serve to illustrate the lack of agility of the Danish film establishment prior to the reforms discussed above.[10] It is important to emphasize that Dogma 95 does not seem to have been conceived as a protest against the state of the Danish film industry per se. For von Trier, frustrated at endless delays over the funding of what would become his pre-Dogma offering, *Breaking the Waves* (1996), Danish film was simply not worth protesting against in 1995. "If you want to protest about something then the thing you're protesting against has to have a certain amount of authority," he told one interviewer resignedly.[11] Nevertheless, the movement had a catalytic effect.

When von Trier first mooted the idea of a series of Dogma 95 films made by Danish directors, an initial promise of investment from the then Danish minister of culture, Jytte Hilden, was waylaid by the Danish Film Institute's insistence on parity of access to state funding for all filmmakers, affiliated to Dogma 95 or not. Logically, this undermined the influence of the Dogma 95 Vow of Chastity, for the film projects would be evaluated not on the basis of their adherence to the vow but according to the criteria laid down by the institute's board. With the issue of funding for Danish cinema a hot potato in the Danish press, a deal to finance the first Dogma films was struck with the Danish Broadcasting Company, Danmarks Radio.[12] One film directed by each of the four members of the Dogma brethren—von Trier, Thomas Vinterberg, Søren Kragh-Jacobsen, and Kristian Levring—would be financed by Danmarks Radio, on the condition that the films would be available for broadcasting on national television within three months of their theatrical release.[13] Peter Schepelern remarks that this unusual arrangement freed the directors from the normal round of approvals of scripts and from consultations with producers, investors, and so on.[14] Nevertheless, it is an exquisite irony that the timing—and ultimately the success—of the Dogma 95 project helped pique public interest in, and thus shape, subsequent reformulations of the revamped Danish Film Institute's funding policy, without, however, having benefited from it.

A second catalytic development to coincide with *Festen* was the foundation of Filmbyen, or Film Town, by Lars von Trier and Peter Aalbæk Jensen. This new center for film production was converted from a disused army barracks in Avedøre, strategically located close to Copenhagen and the nearby Kastrup international airport. Its location, however, is not merely commercially strategic but is also an ideological matter: Film Town is intended to demystify and democratize filmmaking, to be a place where knowledge and expertise is handed down from one generation to the next. The Film Town neighborhood comprises "the entire range of companies, artists and artisans from all aspects of audio-visual activity in a concerted effort aimed at opening the doors wide."[15]

The project description for Open Film Town, dated 1999, envisages that master classes and research material from events held at

Avedøre would be made available on the Internet; tellingly, it is proposed that events be made available in the form of transcripts and images, the possibilities afforded by video streaming and widespread broadband connections still being half a decade away. Nonetheless, the justification for making Film Town "the central site for the discussion of film theory and practice" centers on the catalytic role of Dogma 95 in reconfiguring the relations between media theory and practice: "It is acknowledged internationally that Dogme has resulted in the first interest in and discussion of media theory (a discipline that one would otherwise be inclined to call 'extinct') among artists and professionals for decades.... If an up-to-date forum for discussing the medium belongs anywhere in the world at present, it is surely in the home country of Dogme 95!"[16]

While this claim is a little bombastic—chapter 3 considers the broader contemporary context of critical and popular rumination on the nature of the film medium—it drives home how quickly and thoroughly the catalytic effect of *Festen*'s pioneering work with digital video was grasped and exploited. More than a decade on, these transformative ideals and ambitions are still the lingua franca of Film Town. One Film Town tenant whose web presence illustrates how the founding principles persist in the project's DNA is the Zentropa Post Production Hotel, whose suites can be booked on a short-term basis while a film is in postproduction. The language of the hotel's website engages interest.[17] In parallel to the expertise and equipment the hotel is able to offer, the Danish blurb lays emphasis on the word *hygge*, a term generally acknowledged as an untranslatable amalgam of coziness, well-being, and good company. The peculiarly Danish concept of *hygge* is integral to the philosophy and functioning of the hotel. The doors of the editing suites usually stay open, to facilitate conversation and collaboration. More concretely, the Post Production Hotel was founded on Zentropa's unrivaled expertise in the application of digital video and high-definition (HD) technologies. It is unrivaled, the website was still claiming in 2011, precisely because it dates all the way back to the Dogma 95 films: "We know how to create the appropriate visual experience with HD. We've worked with it so much and for so long that we can see both the goldmines and the pitfalls in it better than most others in the branch. Our vision is keener because of experience." This is a succinct illustration of the protean and transformative impact of *Festen* and the Dogma films within the Danish film industry, both in terms of practice and in terms of self-definition. Conversely, the hotel's account of its own origins alongside Dogma 95 and its hard-won experience of getting good results on a shoestring budget reiterates that the success of Dogma 95 was predicated on "the right people" getting to grips with the right equipment at the right time.

The excitement of new media should not blind us to the craft of the "right people" working with tools that are more traditional but no less seductive. The branch of the Danish film industry whose transformation since the 1980s is perhaps most closely linked to the success of *Festen* is screenwriting. Here, too, we see the characteristic high-wire balancing act between creative chaos and professionalization. Interviewed in 2000, Vinterberg reflected on the rapid and comprehensive change in conditions for Danish scriptwriters since the early 1990s:

> There are far better opportunities now for telling a wide range of stories and for focusing intensely on script-related work. The National Film School's script-writing stream is at this point one of the institution's most important and best-supported programs. It's thriving, and the interest in script-writing is enormous. A new subculture of script-writers has emerged, and the people involved really know how to tell stories, and they're being remunerated

for their work. People are also telling stories that have a broader appeal, so I think the situation has improved quite a lot.[18]

The Danish Film School's contemporary emphasis on the craft of storytelling is in no small way due to the influence of Mogens Rukov, a long-serving member of the faculty and Vinterberg's cowriter on *Festen* and other projects. The recent publication of a biography of Rukov indicates his cultural influence and affords an opportunity not only to recapitulate his contribution to Danish film over four decades but also to reassess the impact of *Festen* on the careers of most of those involved and on Danish film more generally.[19] From the perspective of an industry insider, Rukov perceives an increasingly influential role for the scriptwriter in Danish film and, as a corollary, television. Writers have more clout, but also more responsibility. He dates this slow transformation to the beginning of the 1990s, but he also recognizes the pivotal role of his own internationally successful collaboration with Vinterberg on *Festen*.[20] Paradoxically, observes Rukov, increasing professionalization of screenwriting has also entailed what he sees as increasing "industrialization," or the privileging of certain genres and styles in Danish film and television that generate guaranteed box office or viewing figures: "There are so many checkpoints involved in making a film, so much bureaucracy. 'Such and such sells, so it has to look like that,' can be the consequence. The manuscripts have to be approved and authorized so many times by so many people along the way, and decent ticket sales and industry awards are almost always expected."[21] The collaboration between Rukov and Vinterberg that resulted in the *Festen* screenplay will be discussed in depth in chapter 7. Suffice it to say that Rukov's impressions provide a useful counterpoint to more unequivocally positive takes on the professionalization of the Danish film industry since the 1990s. We now turn to look at the Dogma 95 movement in more detail.

Dogma 95: The Manifesto and Vow of Chastity

Has a film movement ever been dissected more thoroughly than Dogma 95? The more one reads about Dogma 95 or the films it spawned, the more one realizes that it is both deadly serious and playfully ironic, that its rules are both devastatingly effective and puzzlingly arbitrary, and that its films are both avant-garde *experimenta* and profoundly humanist documents.

We shall have cause to examine the content of the Dogma 95 manifesto from different angles in various chapters of this book, and it is reproduced in full in appendix A. For the moment, we need only summarize its key tenets: that previous attempts to revolutionize film had come to nothing; that cinema was drowning under a sea of illusionism and "cosmetics"; that part of the problem was the cult of the "individual" film (i.e., director-led filmmaking); and that the way back to freshness and creativity for the experienced, well-funded filmmaker was to strip the process back to basics. A set of ten regulations—allegedly composed in short order in less than an hour by Vinterberg and von Trier[22]—would guide the director back to an anti-aesthetic, even taste-less, methodology that would "force the truth out of characters and situations," as the manifesto puts it.

Taking the ten rules of the Vow of Chastity one at a time, we can make some immediate observations about their impact on *Festen* as process and product. The intention here is to exemplify how the rules panned out in practice, but also to flesh out our knowledge about the film before discussing it in more depth in later chapters.

1 *Shooting must be done on location. Props and sets must not be brought in (if a particular prop is necessary for the story, a location must be chosen where this prop is to be found).*

Festen was shot in and around the Skjoldenæsholm hotel on the island of Sjælland (Zealand), in the countryside near the town of Ringsted, southwest of Copenhagen. A hotel is, of course, the ideal location for a Dogma film, as it is likely to offer an unrivaled range of supplies and props. After the film was complete, Vinterberg inaugurated a tradition of Dogma filmmakers "confessing" to any sins against the rules. His own rebellions concerned almost exclusively the importation of props such as mobile telephones and clothes. As chapter 5 examines, the hotel proved to be a rich source of artifacts and a satisfyingly complex narrative and physical space.

2 *The sound must never be produced apart from the images or vice versa. (Music must not be used unless it occurs where the scene is being shot.)*
There are two sources of music proper in *Festen*: the singing during dinner and the music box that accompanies the opening and closing titles. Nevertheless, the film presents a complex auditory environment. Sound-producing props such as wineglasses serve some of the function of non-diegetic, atmospheric music. Meanwhile, the limitations placed on sound quality by the need to record sound and image simultaneously are used to advantage insofar as they can produce non-naturalistic, impressionistic sound effects. Sound is covered primarily in chapters 5 and 6.

3 *The camera must be hand-held. Any movement or immobility attainable in the hand is permitted.*
The handheld camera is, arguably, the most obvious "trademark" of Dogma 95, though it has its own heritage, as chapter 4 explores. The palm-size digital cameras used in the shoot, however, afford unrivaled mobility and thus fabricate a very distinctive hotel space, as discussed in chapter 5.

4 *The film must be in color. Special lighting is not acceptable. (If there is too little light for exposure the scene must be cut or a single lamp be attached to the camera.)*

5 *Optical work and filters are forbidden.*

Festen makes gentle sport with the ban on artificial light and optical work, brashly shooting in candlelight, for example, a candle being lit directly in front of the camera during the after-dinner dancing. The director of photography, Anthony Dod Mantle, set the agenda for cinematography within the Dogma constrictions. It was Dod Mantle who established the feasibility of shooting on digital video even in poor lighting and who saw the potential of the disintegrating image to underline the descent into the darkness of family history.

6 *The film must not contain superficial action. (Murders, weapons, etc. must not occur.)*

The sixth rule is perhaps the most cozily Danish of all. Murders and weapons might well be regarded as "superficial action" by the average Dane, but a viewer living in a city where violence is more endemic might find this rule rather culturally myopic, if not quaint. Yet we do well to remember that *Festen*'s plot involves screaming matches, beatings, vigorous sex, heavy drinking, ghostly apparitions, and accusations of incest and abuse. It is very hard to know, then, what this rule actually means or if *Festen* breaks it. It does, however, lead us to consider what is not shown in *Festen*: the moment of sexual abuse. This point is developed further in chapter 6.

7 *Temporal and geographical alienation are forbidden. (That is to say that the film takes place here and now.)*

From the opening trill of Christian's cell phone, we know that this film takes place in the here and now. There is a more or less classical unity of time and space: the story unfolds over an afternoon, evening, and morning. This is not to say, however, that the space is entirely cohesive and coherent, an issue that is investigated in chapter 5. Moreover, the film flirts with temporal alienation during Christian's dream of his dead sister, but employs a sound effect to suture the dream to "real" time. This dream, and the issue of time, is returned to in chapter 9.

8. *Genre movies are not acceptable.*
The knee-jerk reaction to this rule is to observe that Dogma 95 is a self-defining genre from the outset. *Festen* renders this truism problematic, however, because of its origins in the radio confessional, and its afterlife on the stage, as explored in chapters 7 and 8. Vinterberg has commented that this is a bad rule, because it is too unspecific to foster creativity.[23]

9. *The film format must be Academy 35 mm.*
This rule originally concerned the shooting format as well as the distribution format. Vinterberg and Dod Mantle both wanted to shoot on 35mm but switched to digital video for two reasons: cost and feasibility. In the short period between composing the vow and the making of *Festen*, shooting on handheld digital video had become a viable option. As chapters 3 and 6 discuss, this accident of time and technology had implications for the "look" of *Festen*, for the fate of the Dogma movement, for turn-of-the-millennium filmmaking practice, and for public understanding of the digital.

10. *The director must not be credited.*
Festen's wry take on the role of the director is succinctly established by Vinterberg's cameo as a bewildered taxi driver. Dogma's stance on the director's role as it plays out in the context of *Festen* is explored in chapter 2.

As this anecdotal approach demonstrates, the rules are ordered arbitrarily and the import of their content is uneven. They do not easily translate into the structure of this book, and I have paid little heed to them as an ordering principle. Rather, I draw on the content of the rules as, and when, it is relevant to the discussion at hand.

Rules, Realism, and the "Real" in 1990s Denmark

The difficulty in using the rules as a structuring principle is not just a problem for the author. It is symptomatic of a deeper truth about the Dogma 95 vow, specifically its radical contingency. Any set of rules would, potentially, have had the same effect and impact on filmmaking, or a completely different impact. The rules that we have are slippery, arbitrary, and fundamentally meaningless. That is the very point. However, that the rules seem random and arbitrary does not mean that they lack impact. The rules that happened to crystallize in the Dogma 95 manifesto and vow can also be understood, as Mette Hjort puts it, as "multiply motivated" by the Dogma brethren's wish to take away the tools they themselves found most useful and to legitimize the less cost-intensive modes of production that characterize the cinema of small nations.[24]

I would, though, like to complement Hjort's argument about the multiple motivations of the Dogma 95 vow with the observation that the studied arbitrariness of the Dogma 95 rules is in itself not arbitrary but culturally contingent. To be sure, the publication of manifestos had previously been an established practice for von Trier and other avant-garde filmmakers, and Dogma 95 must be understood in the context of von Trier's career. However, there is a broader sociocultural context that is rarely, if ever, mentioned as a constituent element of the late-twentieth-century culture from which Dogma 95 emerged: the formal breakthrough. This term is used in literary and cultural studies to describe the extraordinary degree of experimentation in form that characterized Danish literature and art in the 1990s. Crucially, these experiments with formal frameworks can be seen as a response to anxieties about representation and "the real." To adopt a metaphor from the Danish critic Erik Skyum-Nielsen, the Danish novel both imploded and exploded in that decade.[25] It imploded into super-short text fragments, often called *kortprosa* (short prose), or it exploded into sweeping, encyclopedic epics, which were often themselves complex, nonlinear experiments in literary chronology and causality. Analogous experiments in form also manifested themselves in the context of postmodernist (or post-historical) historiography.[26] Such histories aim to disrupt the narrative chains of cause and effect, which inculcate a sense of "rightness" or "fatedness" about the order of events. By recounting events nonchronologically, in fragments, or from the perspective of hitherto "silent" individuals, this kind of historical "tale" tries to reveal the contingency and chaos lurking under conventional historical or nationalist narratives. It also reminds us that the line between history and story, between "fact" and "fiction," is impossible to trace with absolute certainty. Serendipitously, in Danish, the word *historie* has a double meaning: it is both "history" and "story." As our discussion of *Festen* develops, we shall see that the ambivalent distinction between "history" and "story" resonates both with the ontological and ethical ambitions of the Dogma 95 movement and with the origins of *Festen* itself. In the Dogma 95 manifesto's stated objective of "forcing the truth out of characters and situations" we hear the echo of that postmodern anxiety about the constructedness of histories and stories: Who is allowed to speak? Is there really any truth to be forced out of a situation?

Arguably, then, in the Dogma 95 manifesto's exhortation to the filmmaker to capture "the instant" and treat it as "more important than the whole," there lies not only the longing for (analogue) film's indexical certainty, its ability to guarantee that this moment actually occurred and has been registered, but also a post-historical suspicion that the moment is etiolated in its incorporation into a meaningful narrative. Forbidding the manipulation of the recorded moment in postproduction reduces the risk that its "truth" can be tampered with. In the case of Dogma 95, the rules in the vow are the formal experiment that gives access to "the real" by breaking through the conventions of "realism," especially those related to narrative and space.

Indeed, Dogma 95 is one of the artistic expressions of what Britta Timm Knudsen and Bodil Marie Thomsen describe as a "hunger for reality" in Danish and international culture around the turn of the millennium.[27] Dogma 95, like reality television, performance art, and formally experimental literature of the 1990s, was engaged in exploring the liminal spaces between "reality" and "media," "documentary" and "fiction," "representation" and "simulation."[28] In particular, Knudsen and Thomsen argue, new media afforded possibilities for rethinking the notion of "event." While postmodernist art of the 1980s was characterized by the logic of the copy, the mirror, the labyrinth, and metatextual commentary, in the 1990s the emphasis shifted to movement, action, event, and the production of affect. In both decades, the role of the viewer or reader in the co-creation of the text was paramount, but the 1990s saw a renegotiation of the concept of realism; the works now appealed to the viewer to enter into an "affective contract" through strategies of pathos, shock, or marked reference to the senses.[29] As Thomsen writes of von Trier's only Dogma film, *Idioterne* (The Idiots; 1998), the strategy is to create reality, produce an event, by inciting the viewer to participate affectively. The issue of realism in this context, argues Thomsen, can best be tackled by posing questions such as "was it intense?" and "did it provoke new thoughts?" rather than assessing verisimilitude or coherence of plot.[30]

The issues of technology, affect, and the senses in *Festen* are returned to in part 2 of this book, though the notion runs throughout the discussion. For the moment, it can be reiterated that Dogma 95, in its conception and its effects, can be contextualized as one expression of a broader interest in formal experimentation and new iterations of "realism" across a variety of media in 1990s Denmark and beyond.

Identity and Nationalism in 1990s Denmark

The turn to radical uncertainty in historiography and formal experimentation at the end of the 1990s was partly symptomatic of an ongoing interrogation of Danish identity among intellectuals and more populist sources alike. It would be several years before the 2006 crisis triggered by the publication in a Danish newspaper of cartoons of the prophet Muhammad would sweep the globe. But Denmark, in the mid- to late 1990s, was engaged in a collective renegotiation of what it meant to be Danish in the face of globalization, European economic and political integration, and increasingly visible immigration. When pressed on the issue of whether the overt episodes of racism in *Festen* against Helene's black American boyfriend are intended as a commentary on contemporary social attitudes in Denmark, Vinterberg has sometimes answered in the affirmative: "It's true that I thought to myself early on in the process that it would be wonderful if the film in some strange way could be a portrait of Denmark. . . . By including, for example, a foreign element—a black man who speaks a different language—it's possible, in a very banal way, suddenly to underscore the extent to which the film's depiction of the family functions as a portrait of Denmark."[31] The allegorical reading of *Festen* as the family as national synecdoche, with Gbatokai as the ethnic outsider, is a compelling one. For example, Jack Stevenson sees the "national" family in *Festen* as "riven with class antagonisms":

> The father, Helge, can be seen as "the establishment," the corporation in all its power and arrogance. The mother, Elsa [sic], is the loyal and trusting "silent majority," her impervious smile repelling all doubts in the cause of preserving the status quo. Oldest brother, Christian, is the dissident expatriate who has renounced his citizenship and left the country. And then there is the younger brother, Michael, who owns a "bistro" (probably a ratty bar).... He represents the lower classes. His sister, Helene, is the politically correct intellectual.[32]

If nothing else, the notion that the family constitutes a national allegory would explain the extraordinary range of language varieties used by the members of the family; Michael in particular speaks in a strong Copenhagen sociolect that belies his supposed boarding-school education. In fact, language is a subtle locus of tension in the film, functioning to problematize the notion of belonging. On the one hand, Michael's slangy drawl is accepted without remark by his family. On the other hand, the occasional grammatical mistakes made by German toastmaster Helmut are publicly policed and corrected by partygoers (a national habit that will be recognizable to anyone who has learned Danish as a second language). Conversely, Else harnesses her inability to pronounce Gbatokai's name into a snide attempt at domesticating, or culturally assimilating, the foreigner, referring to him first as "Gonzales" and then shortening his name to the Danish man's name Kai. This incident provokes laughter from the guests.

Should the viewer spontaneously laugh, he or she is implicated in the mocking collective, complicit in the shared knowledge that the joke rests on the apparent ridiculousness of the idea that a black man might bear the name Kai.

Indeed, it is in his potential to push the viewer to interrogate his or her own response to the behavior of the collective in the film that I think Gbatokai functions most powerfully. In other words, looking at this character through the lens of the "new Danish realism," as discussed above, gives us a sharper set of tools to understand his impact than if we were to treat him merely as a cipher for outsiderness. A second example of Gbatokai's affective impact centers on that potent indicator of national belonging: the incorporated collective memory of popular song.[33] Much has been made of the manipulation of the extras in *Festen*, who were not forewarned of the content of Christian's revelatory speech and had no idea how to react.[34] However, it is striking that the extras, as a group, do not shrink from enthusiastically singing along with Michael when he launches into a racist song to bait Gbatokai. I do not mean to suggest here that the actors or extras (as opposed to the fictional characters) are racist. However, if the singsong was set up according to the same principles as the speech scene—that is, if the extras were manipulated to hover uneasily between reacting spontaneously and remaining "in character"—then this group performance scene can also be construed as a kind of film-sociological experiment. How will a group respond to an ethically questionable stimulus? For a viewer steeped in Danish tradition, the intensity of this scene might provoke the ambivalent experience of feeling shocked at the group's behavior, while realizing that he or she also knows the words to the racist song and is thus implicated in the same cultural grouping.

The import of Gbatokai's character, then, stems less from his symbolic or allegorical status as the racial and linguistic outsider and more from the potential his presence provides for intensification of the viewer's affective response to the film. Racism is rendered visible, audible, and thus palpable; the viewer's affective response (crystallizing into horror or, feasibly, conspiratorial delight) justifies his presence, regardless of how well-rounded we might consider his character to be.[35]

There is an interesting cultural and political footnote to the issue of turn-of-the-millennium nationalism, in which *Festen* has a bit part, both as a Dogma film and as a Danish work of art. In 2006, the then Danish minister of culture, Brian Mikkelsen, launched his prize project, the Danish Cultural Canon. Intended both as a primer in the Danish cultural heritage and as a starting point for debate, the canon features a list of key works in each of nine art forms, ranging from architecture to film. Each list was selected by a panel of experts, and their choices were published in coffee-table book format and online. The exercise was not without controversy. The most vehement cry of resistance came from von Trier, who declared that if one of his films should be included in the canon, he would burn the Danish flag in the parking lot of his film production company. Inevitably, von Trier's contribution to the Dogma 95 stable, *Idioterne*, was included by the judges in the canon. In response, von Trier thought better of an act of flag burning and undertook instead to make a short "video greeting" (*videohilsen*) to Mikkelsen, in which he cuts the white cross out of the flag to make a red flag of revolution and exhorts the minister to "cultivate the nation—don't nationalize culture!"[36] We might muse that *Festen*, also included in the canon, already contained its own more subtle protest against what von Trier identified as a swelling tide of popular and state jingoism, in the person of Gbatokai and the hostility he triggers among the party guests.

Conclusion

Festen gave form to a hitherto untested cinematic document, the Dogma 95 Manifesto and Vow of Chastity, which provided a set of creative constraints for the film. *Festen* and Dogma 95 emerged in the midst of a period of reorganization and renewed confidence for the Danish film industry. Dogma exerted its own catalytic effect on the Danish film industry, but must be seen as one of several factors—including the creative leadership of von Trier—that conspired to produce a sea change in Danish film production. The rules associated with Dogma 95, and their expression in *Festen*, can also be understood in the broader context of 1990s Danish art and culture, with its focus on formal experimentation and new forms of realism that implicate the viewer affectively in the textual event. Lastly, *Festen* was not immune from sociopolitical anxieties about national identity and belonging that inflected much cultural output in Denmark in the 1990s. We can see its inclusion of an ethnic outsider in its cast of characters as one example of how the film harnesses the affective response of the viewer in order to, as Dogma 95 mandates, "force the truth from characters and situations."

2

The Auteur and Cinema History

Festen cowriter Mogens Rukov, in his compelling, staccato style, reminisces about the reception of the film at Cannes in 1998, where it was awarded the Special Jury Prize:

April 98. Cannes film festival. We are in the official competition. We and *The Idiots* by Lars von Trier. I walk the red carpet of the Grand Palais twice this week. This is not the biggest experience. No, the biggest experience is the applause.

It's not just a big applause. It's imperial. We are sitting in the big hall. There are about 3,000 people dressed in evening dress; they are in black, very elegant. The film ends. The lights go up. The applause starts. It does not end. It continues. They applaud for 11 minutes. They approach us. Slowly. They encircle us. They are on the balcony, in the pit and coming closer. A beautiful view, *le monde* encircling, *décolletage*. I like women's bodies.

I am a smoker. I wish they would stop applauding. I want to have a cigarette. But they continue the applause. This started in a kitchen and some offices, not very elegant offices, no celebrated condition. It comes out as this. Thomas gives 250 interviews in the next two days, I think.[1]

Dogma 95, we might say, was always international, or at least European, in its ambition; after all, Lars von Trier had launched Dogma 95 in Paris some three years earlier. But it is those "imperial" waves of applause for *Festen* that initiate Dogma 95 into international cinema history. Or, as Mette Hjort puts it: "It is important to note that Dogma 95 has itself been globalized since 1995, when the blueprint was first made public, Vinterberg's success at Cannes in 1998 having done much to imbue the concept with a kind of accelerative force."[2] By all accounts, Vinterberg himself was subjected to no mean "accelerative force," reportedly undertaking hundreds of interviews in the wake of Cannes alone and then spending an extended period engaged in traveling the globe to promote the film.

All of this is the logical corollary of the success of a movement that explicitly sets out to resist global tendencies in film. Dogma 95 was not simply a response to the socioeconomics of contemporary film culture but also a reaction against key tenets of international film theory and history. This chapter considers how Dogma 95 explicitly contextualizes itself in cinema culture, as well as some of its implicit or incidental film-historical relationships.

Dogma 95 in Cinema History

Before examining the manifesto itself, we can note that the decision to launch Dogma 95 at the celebration of the centenary of cinema invites reflection on whether the twentieth century's last film movement implicitly understands itself as marking the end of one century and inaugurating the next. The manifesto gives no explicit indication that it defines itself in relation to early cinema. However, Dogma 95 has assumed, post hoc, at least tangential relevance to two cyclical models of cinema history. First, the meme of the "second golden age of Danish Cinema" posits Dogma as a trigger in returning Danish cinema to its former glory. Second, as some of the earliest commercially successful examples of digital filmmaking, *Festen* and other key Dogma films are caught up in another cyclical understanding of film history: the argument that the digital era restores cinematic "spectacle" to some semblance of the dominance it enjoyed in the era that Tom Gunning christens the "cinema of attractions" (roughly 1895–1906).[3] We need to be careful with this line of thought, however; the spectacular images and experiences that computer-generated cinema makes possible are the very antithesis of Dogma. This paradox is emphasized by Lev Manovich in his discussion of the relations between cinema and new media. For Manovich, Dogma 95 films were nothing less than "reactions to the increasing reliance of cinema on computer techniques in postproduction" (though the Dogma 95 manifesto does not explicitly decry the use of computer technology).[4] Manovich's project is to trace the return of the "repressed of the cinema," that is, the reemergence in digital cinema of animation, special effects, and the "manual construction of images," techniques that had been pushed to the margins of cinema by the dominance of live-action filmmaking.[5] Seen from this perspective, Dogma 95's adoption of digital video to make "lens-based recordings of reality . . . to make art out of a footprint," in the manner of what Manovich calls live-action film, is at best incidental, at worst counterintuitive to the project.[6] Thus, although Dogma 95 pioneered the use of digital video cameras in shooting feature films, it connects the films only circumstantially to other techniques of the digital age such as computer-generated imagery (CGI).

Manovich's interest in how media conventions crystallize would surely lead him to concede, however, that Dogma 95 at least problematizes many of the formal and narrative norms of twentieth-century cinema, if not its indexical underpinnings. For example, Ian Conrich and Estella Tincknell have argued for an understanding of Dogma as a "post-Institutional Mode of Representation," that is, as rejecting and reworking many of the building blocks of film language that had been established by around 1919: "Dogma's rejection of film's formal precision is both a stripping back to the improvisation, resourcefulness and immediacy of much of early cinema, and an excoriation of the conventions of a prevailing film-making practice which has manufactured conformity to a series of recognised stylistic and aesthetic procedures."[7] We might also point to a more tenuous similarity between *Festen* and early cinema: the uncertainty of subjects faced with an unfamiliar apparatus. In early cinema, people are frequently caught staring at the unfamiliar camera; in Dogma, actors and extras are reported to have been less than sure about how they should react to this new and discomfitingly miniature camera.[8]

However, while the logic of the ten rules of the Vow of Chastity is indeed suggestive of an unspoken desire to rebuild film language from its beginnings, the most blatant intertext of the Dogma 95 manifesto is, of course, the French New Wave:

> DOGMA 95 is a collective of film directors founded in Copenhagen in spring 1995.
>
> DOGMA 95 has the expressed goal of countering "certain tendencies" in the cinema today.
>
> DOGMA 95 is a rescue action!
>
> In 1960 enough was enough! The movie was dead and called for resurrection. The goal was correct but the means were not! The new wave proved to be a ripple that washed ashore and turned to muck.

Slogans of individualism and freedom created works for a while, but no changes. The wave was up for grabs, like the directors themselves. The wave was never stronger than the men behind it. The anti-bourgeois cinema itself became bourgeois, because the foundations upon which its theories were based was the bourgeois perception of art. The auteur concept was bourgeois romanticism from the very start and thereby . . . false!

To DOGMA 95 cinema is not individual!

As if pinpointing the year 1960 was not explicit enough, these opening paragraphs of the Dogma 95 manifesto play on three instantly recognizable tropes associated with the Nouvelle Vague: François Truffaut's 1954 essay for the journal *Cahiers du cinéma*, titled "Une certaine tendance du cinéma français" (A Certain Tendency in French Film); Jean-Luc Godard's increasingly virulent stance against "bourgeois" cinema; and the very metaphor of a "wave," which is, here, rather scatologically developed as "a ripple that washed ashore and turned to muck."[9] It quickly transpires that the real target is the concept of the director as *auteur*: the New Wave's notion of the director as the single creative genius—or, at least, an artist with an identifiable "style"—behind any given work. The antidote to auteur cinema, at least for the cosignatories of the Dogma 95 manifesto, is to "swear as a director to refrain from personal taste!" and to renounce their status as artists. A great deal of ink has been spilled puzzling out the intent of the manifesto: was it serious, or was it a bout of ironic postulating? That Vinterberg and von Trier sign the very document in which they swear to refrain from being credited as directors establishes from the outset that Dogma 95 is, as the responses (quoted verbatim here and below) to the list of frequently asked questions (FAQs) on its now-defunct website insist, a deadly serious exercise dripping with irony:

There is an implicit duplicity in The Dogme95 Manifesto. On one hand it contains a deep irony and on the other it is most serious meant. Irony and seriousness is interlinked in inseparable. What we have concerned ourselves with is the making of a set of rules. In this sense it is a kind of play, a game called "rule-making." Seriousness and play go hand in hand. A clear example of this is that the very strict and serious Dogme95 Manifesto was actually written in only 25 minutes and under continuous bursts of merry laughter. . . . Still, we maintain that we are in earnest. Dogme is not for fun. It is, however, both liberating, merry and almost fun to work under such a strict set of rules. It is this duplicity which is the magic of "dogme."[10]

The knowing duplicity extends to the attitude toward auteurism. Von Trier has commented that the ban on crediting the director, and the rules in general, should be seen as "a punch in the face of all directors," but that this need not prevent Dogma films from reflecting the styles of their respective directors.[11]

As a coauthor and signatory of the Dogma 95 Manifesto and Vow of Chastity, alongside von Trier, Vinterberg was already more notorious than the other Dogma brethren (namely, Kristian Levring and Søren Kragh-Jacobsen), or later directors of Dogma films. While it was von Trier who flamboyantly launched the movement's founding texts in Paris, Vinterberg's authority to discuss and explain the genesis and intentions of the project was widely accepted. It is telling, for example, that clarification of the intended scope of the tenth rule, in the Dogme95.dk FAQs, is provided by Vinterberg (who in fact seems to have been responsible for most of the site's textual content):

> *The Vow of Chastity states that the director must not be credited—isn't it contradictory or ironic then that the dogme*

> *directors do give interviews and that the PR surrounding the films is so intense?*
>   The Dogme 95 Manifesto is exclusively aimed at the filmmaking process ("the making of") and not the "afterlife"—e.g. pr, marketing and distribution—of the films. The "dogme" rules should be considered "symbolic" and not as a means to remaining secretive or hidden. They are an expression of the director's wish to recede into the background and thus push other talent into the foreground. The "dogme" director's finest duty is to register private moments between persons and not to influence them.[12]

That the film industry and media—Dogma included—do not have mechanisms to distribute, promote, or discuss films without recourse to the figure of the director shows just how deeply the influence of this role has taken root in the profession and in the popular imagination.

On one level, then, the inherent irony is flagged by the "knowing" signatures, which thrust the "invisible" directors into the spotlight as Dogma brethren, years before any of the films made under the Dogma label appeared. Granted, the films were policed for any trace of the director's name in the credits, and a (signed) Dogma 95 certificate flashed up at the beginning of the film instead. But there was no attempt to hide the identity of the directors from the press or public; in the majority of contexts the convention has been to credit the Dogma 95 directors in standard terms. Vinterberg has admitted that his cameo role as a taxi driver in *Festen* constituted a knowing admission of defeat on the issue of obliterating the director's influence.[13] But it is also a nod to, for example, Alfred Hitchcock's habit of appearing in his own films. Here, the Dogma manifesto presents us with a second layer of paradox concerning the issue of the filmmaker. The manifesto bans the individual director from being credited or exercising personal taste, ostensibly in order to resist the overblown and misleading concept of the auteur. Nevertheless, in positioning itself as emanating from a group of directors reacting to earlier movements in film history, Dogma 95 inserts its own authors within what Roland Barthes calls a "process of filiation," in which each oeuvre is understood to be influenced by authored works anterior to it.[14] Thus the role of the director as intellectually and ideologically ambitious cinephile is reiterated, and his "influences" are picked over in ways that, again, redouble the focus on the director.

Nevertheless, perhaps we might muse that the tenth rule is, precisely, the *tenth* rule because the other nine have already done its work. Berys Gaut has argued that while the tenth rule can only be considered symbolic, the majority of other rules in the vow have the effect of constraining the director's ability to "force a possibly idiosyncratic vision onto reality."[15] Mette Hjort has undertaken a painstaking investigation into how the rules affect the influence and agency of the other members of the filmmaking team in the context of Lone Scherfig's *Italiensk for begyndere* (Italian for Beginners; 2000).[16] The tenth rule, then, playfully draws attention to the problematics of auteurship and the impossibility of surmounting its power; it throws up an ironic smokescreen behind which the practitioners can puzzle out how to do the heavy lifting of collaborative creativity in genuinely new ways.

Vinterberg and Rukov's compelling account of the creative process behind the screenplay indirectly corroborates this attribution of collective—yet unwitting—alchemy. The cowriters' short epilogue to the Danish edition of the *Festen* screenplay, first published in Danish in 1998, is as much a meditation on the symbiosis between scriptwriter, director, editor, and actors as it is a synopsis of the transition of *Festen* from idea to manuscript to screen. On a more general level, of particular interest are Vinterberg and Rukov's remarks on the implicit balance of power between writer and director, as well

2.1   Thomas Vinterberg's cameo as a hapless taxi driver

as the other actors in the creative process.[17] Aside from the unspoken division of labor according to which Vinterberg took care of the characters and Rukov looked after the film's narrative dynamism, Rukov was also aware, as screenwriter, that even his best ideas might never make it onto film during the production process. They might not get committed to film, or they might get edited out. Editor Valdís Óskarsdóttir—praised as brilliant by Rukov—brings to bear her mastery of the new technology to enable Vinterberg and Rukov to try out different versions of the story in moments, so that what is edited out is still there, but in a better form. Nevertheless, the cowriters' conclusion to this discussion is that "somehow, the film always belongs to the director. Even at the manuscript stage."[18] With that, we now turn to look at the shape of Vinterberg's career as a Dogma 95 auteur.

THE AUTEUR AND CINEMA HISTORY   45

Vinterberg as Auteur

If, as Linda Haverty Rugg has argued, Ingmar Bergman functioned as the model for the French New Wave's definition of an auteur, Vinterberg's fate has been to have auteur status thrust upon him and then suffer constant speculation as to how he would continue to fulfill the job description.[19]

Vinterberg's public persona as director was crystallized by his involvement with Dogma 95 and has been constructed in the media over two decades as a teleology of (unfulfilled) brilliance and potential; the shape of his career is always already under review, while it is unfolding. Vinterberg's career, and the case of *Festen* in particular, provides fertile ground for an examination of the problematics of the auteur.

It is notable that the Danish press already had its eye on Vinterberg before he had made a feature film. His first prize was the 1994 Natsværmerpris (literally, the Moth Prize), awarded annually to a promising Danish film talent. His short film *Sidste omgang* (Last Round; 1993) had won the prize for best graduation work at the International Film School Festival in Munich, and these prizes attracted the attention of Denmark's quality daily newspaper, *Politiken*. Vinterberg then made a short fiction film, *Drengen der gik baglæns* (The Boy Who Walked Backwards; 1994), and his first feature, *De største helte* (The Greatest Heroes; 1996). By this time he had become a founding signatory to the Dogma 95 manifesto, which would shape his second feature film, *Festen*. It is particularly instructive, however, to consider two of the productions that followed *Festen* and the media discourses that floated in their wake.

The immediate successor to *Festen*, *It's All about Love*, did not premiere until 2003, leaving plenty of time for press and critical speculation. The film is a futuristic ice-skating adventure set in a time of catastrophic climate change, cloning, and diseases of the heart. Vinterberg describes the point of the film as follows:

> The film is primarily about modern people who are in constant motion, and never really present. The modern individual who is sitting at home with his family thinking about work, and who then goes to work and misses his family. His nearest and dearest in reality are workmates, because they're all there most of the time, that's their experience most of the time. They're not rooted in a particular geographical place because they're moving around all the time on their laptops, and thus they're everywhere at once without being anywhere.[20]

Unsurprisingly, the film fell victim to discourses according to which it was evaluated against Vinterberg-as-auteur and *Festen*-as-forerunner. As a film title, *It's All about Love* might be suspected of mocking the saccharine popular discourse of "love" as universal panacea and ubiquitous narrative theme. A knowing wink, perhaps, to a newfound freedom from the vow's eighth rule forbidding genre movies, or a post hoc interpretation of *Festen* itself? The press interviews publicizing *It's All about Love*, however, tended toward a biographical explanation. In the years after the international success of *Festen*, Vinterberg found himself caught up in a coldly cosmopolitan and peripatetic lifestyle. That Vinterberg's auteur persona is both charismatic and generously unreclusive makes it hard to disentangle *It's All about Love* as a text from its biographical function in the trajectory of his career. *It's All about Love* was, inevitably, received—and only rarely acclaimed—as the anti-*Festen*, and by all accounts it made little impact either "at home" in Denmark or abroad.[21] What is interesting about Vinterberg's own pronouncements on *It's All about Love* is that he repeatedly cites it as the film that is closest to him, but sees it as a "problem child." In his flight from the Dogma 95 aesthetic, Vinterberg's intention with this film was to give it an "illusionary" look—again, the "opposite of Dogme" is invoked by the director in the DVD voice-over commentary—to the extent that what was shot on location was recolored to resemble studio work and what was shot in a studio was retouched to approach the on-location shots. It seems that the illusionary or painterly effect that Vinterberg was striving for had much to do with an urge to represent digital morphing and representation itself, gesturing both into and beyond the medium of film, a strategy that is also implicated in Vinterberg's description of the film's internal logic as more like a painting than like a narrative.[22] Far away, and yet not so far away, from *Festen*—and yet the film was critiqued for not being *Festen*.

It's All about Love was followed by *Dear Wendy* (2005), a cowboy-style piece written by von Trier, and then by the light comedy *En mand kommer hjem* (A Man Comes Home; 2007). The title of the latter, ironically, has been seized upon (along with *The Boy Who Walked Backwards*) in reviews of Vinterberg's career. When *A Man Comes Home* turned out not to be a "homecoming" for the promise of *Festen*, the metaphor was again trotted out in relation to Vinterberg's next film, *Submarino* (2010). An adaptation of Jonas T. Bengtsson's novel of the same name, shot on 16mm, and, notably, featuring several first-time actors among the cast, *Submarino* tracks two estranged brothers in their respective flights from a violent and tragic childhood.

The premiere of *Submarino* in spring 2010 unleashed a kind of midterm retrospective of Vinterberg's work, not least after it won the Nordic Council Film Prize. The associated interviews and reviews are useful in contextualizing *Festen* twelve years on—precisely because *Submarino* is painted as a "return to form" after a decade during which none of Vinterberg's output allegedly matched up to his international breakthrough film. There is a trope in the reviews of *Submarino* that is made most explicit by Bo Green Jensen in his film review and interview with Vinterberg from March 2010: the review is titled "Redux," suggesting that Vinterberg's form has been "restored," presumably to the *Festen* era, while the interview plays on the film title *The Boy Who Walked Backwards* to describe the director's career. *Submarino*, thinks Green Jensen, is reminiscent of "Kieslowski before the aestheticization took over. Vinterberg before the success set in. In any case this fable on the beautiful losers in northwestern [Copenhagen] is the director's most perfectly sculpted film in living memory."[23] Thus the shape of Vinterberg's career is always already being reviewed, even compared to itself, as above, and *Festen* still haunts his work. For example, anecdotally, at the question and answer session following the London Film Festival screening of *Submarino* in October 2010, some of the questioners in the audience were under the impression that *Submarino* was a Dogma 95 film. At the time of my writing this book, Vinterberg's *Jagten* (The Hunt) has been announced as "in competition" at the 2012 Cannes Film Festival. This news has prompted the Danish Film Institute to observe that not since *Festen* in 1998 has there been a Danish-language film in the main competition at Cannes (though five English-language films by von Trier have competed during that period).[24] The international theatrical release of *Jagten* in late 2012 may yet trigger a flurry of reviews writing this new film into the post-*Festen* mythology.

Vinterberg admits to Green Jensen in a recent interview that the ten years after *Festen* saw him fumbling, desperately trying to escape from a promise to which the world wanted to hold him. Asked whether the success of *Festen* had become an albatross around his neck, Vinterberg answers: "Definitely yes. It has been a blessing and a curse. And mostly the latter."[25] How Vinterberg has recently tried to overcome this burden is discussed in chapter 8.

Conclusion

Festen's glittering reception on the global stage was the fulfillment of Dogma 95's explicit engagement with international cinema history. The manifesto and Vow of Chastity spar with globally accepted cinematic norms and tendencies and with the critical-theoretical tradition of politically inflected manifestos and movements. As a document signed by a group of directors, the Dogma 95 manifesto's interest in combating the bourgeois notion of the auteur can only be understood ironically. The manifesto, in conjunction with the vow's tenth rule, specifying that the director not be credited, fosters rather than precludes a context in which Vinterberg has been constructed in the press as the epitome of an *auteur*. The reception of Vinterberg's works has exhibited a distinctive tendency to comment on the shape of his career while it is unfolding, with *Festen* as an early masterpiece against which his later films are inevitably measured and found wanting.

3

Dogma 95 and the Death of Film

If, in the future, film is shot on [digital] video completely, and someone looks to your film as "the death of film," how would you respond to that?
VINTERBERG: I would feel responsible. And I would be very sad. It's of course not going to happen.
—Jeremy Lehrer, "Denmark's DV Director"

The twentieth century began with futuristic utopias and dreams of unending development and ended with nostalgia and quests for restoration.
—Svetlana Boym, "The Off-Modern Mirror"

The French film history against which Dogma 95 explicitly defined itself had one final twist to offer—also in 1998. Between the Dogma manifesto's allusion to the Nouvelle Vague in 1995 and the premiere of *Festen*, Jean-Luc Godard had completed his *Histoire(s) du cinéma* (1998), an ambitious video project, begun a decade earlier, that explores cinema as the twentieth century's own medium. Embedded in the French title of the project are two ambiguities: the word "histoire" translates into English as both "history" and "story," and the "s" in parentheses evokes the possibility that both "history" and "story" are multiple. (As we know from chapter 1, the Danish noun "historie(r)" contains the same semantic possibilities.) If the French New Wave had been the midcentury cinema movement par excellence, here, at the end of the century, its chief architect was still entirely in tune with the times in his insistence on cinema as a collective, fragmented, nonlinear (hi)story.

Writing in 2006, Laura Mulvey muses that by the end of the twentieth century, "new technologies opened up new perceptual possibilities, new ways of looking, not at the world, but at the internal world of cinema. The century had accumulated a recorded film world, like a parallel universe, that can now be halted or slowed or fragmented."[1] The technology that made Godard's project feasible was video, enabling him to "cite" and visually juxtapose fragments of the century's film archive. But the digital revolution that would even more radically alter the viewer's relationship to cinema, and with which Dogma 95 would come to be popularly associated, was already under way. Like video, digital filmmaking enhanced the mobility of the filmmaker, the instantaneity of information exchange, and the manipulability of the image. But so, too, did the digital inherit from its video predecessor the stain of an ambivalent relationship to the moment or event it records. We now turn to look at how Dogma 95 and *Festen* were imbricated in this latest chapter in the (hi)story of the cinema.

The "Death" of Film and the Digital "Revolution"

"Suddenly," writes Mulvey of the mid-1990s, "the cinema seemed to age."[2] On the one hand, this was an effect of the vertigo of historical perspective: the centenary of the Lumière brothers' inaugural screening in Paris unleashed a frenzy of intellectual debate on the metamorphoses of the medium during its first century. As we have seen, the Dogma 95 manifesto was itself a symptom of this moment of reflection on the shape of film history, in its allusions to other times and movements, and Godard was already in on the act. On the other hand, film scholars were taking stock not only in historiographical terms but also in a more material sense: a century of wear and tear had taken its toll on the cinematic archive. By the mid-1990s, cinema conservationists were warning in apocalyptic terms of the fundamental ephemerality of the medium. Nowhere is the impossibility of preserving the global film archive laid out more starkly than in the impertinent essay by an anonymous (fictional?) peer reviewer of Paolo Cherchi Usai's *The Death of Cinema*. This essay states the case boldly: the unfathomable proliferation of films made worldwide, and the failure to find a reliably sustainable successor material to nitrate stocks, renders the long-term preservation of a representative selection of film output fundamentally impossible. The advent of the digital, warns the essay, must not be seen as a panacea: the sustainability of digital methods of storage and distribution of cinema will only be tried and tested over time.[3]

Nevertheless, Mulvey identifies the U.S. launch of the DVD format in March 1997 as the birth of an irrevocably new era:

> The resonance of ageing, and of death, associated with the cinema's centenary coincided with the arrival of a technology that

created a divide between the "old" and the "new" media. However significant the development of video had been for film, the fact that all forms of information and communication can now be translated into binary coding with a single system signals more precisely the end of an era. The specificity of cinema, the relation between its material base and its poetics, dissolves while other relations, intertextual and cross-media, begin to emerge.[4]

Mulvey's identification of March 1997 as the watershed privileges digital distribution as the turning point for the cinema. James Monaco's timeline of the late 1990s corroborates this date, though he specifies that the computing and entertainment industries had agreed on standards for the new DVD format in September 1995.[5] In spring 1996, a commentator in *Film Quarterly* was pondering whether consumers would really shell out for yet another new format that would do nothing to resolve the debate between "pro- and anti-home video factions" of the film community.[6] Again, we see how the 1995–98 period straddles the start of an unexpectedly radical sea change in the behavior of film consumers.

We might also look to the impact of digital technology on the production process as a harbinger of a new era. Monaco and David Rodowick agree on the mid-1990s as the time that digital nonlinear editing systems really began to be perceived as the industry standard, having gradually replaced mechanical editing tables since the late 1980s.[7] When *Festen* made it to Valdís Óskarsdóttir's editing desk in late 1997, Vinterberg's cowriter, Mogens Rukov, was bowled over by the ease with which different scenarios could be tested using what he called "a wonderfully clever electronic picturetypewriter, an Awid."[8] Rukov's ingenious neologism for Avid digital nonlinear editing equipment is perhaps a case of gently self-deprecating Luddism, but also an expression of quite how novel digital editing still was in the mid- to late 1990s.

The digital revolution was felt not only at the production and distribution stage; its effects on consumption are still just beginning to be understood. Central to Mulvey's 2006 book is the effect of digital storage and distribution on the viewer's relation to, or, more precisely, consumption of, the film text. While videotape brought the advantages of portability, affordability, and rewindability to every study, it is the DVD that has revolutionized our relationship to the film as text. Mulvey identifies the nonlinear access to the film afforded by the DVD as the key development: the abilities to consume the film in chapters and to still the moving image at will are profoundly new ways of interacting with the film. For Mulvey, the "technological uncanny" of a medium not yet quite understood goes hand in hand with a "technological curiosity" never quite sated by DVD paratexts such as "making of" documentaries, outtakes, and interviews.[9] These developments have broader ramifications than our leisure-time habits. In changing how we consume the cinema, they also transform how film mediates the world for us: "Changes in the technologies of seeing affect human perception. As so many theorists and film-makers argued in the 1920s, the cinema, with its mechanical eye, embodied ways in which modernity had transformed perception. Now, as the digital affects contemporary perception of the world, so it also affects popular experience of film and the mode of perception traditionally associated with it."[10]

Steven Shaviro, writing a few years later, in 2010, succinctly expresses how the impact of technological change has outpaced our comprehension and language: "Digital technologies, together with neoliberal economic relations, have given birth to radically new ways of manufacturing and articulating lived experience . . . developments that are so new and unfamiliar that we scarcely have the vocabulary to describe them, and yet that have become so common, and so ubiquitous, that we tend not even to notice them any longer."[11]

For Shaviro, cultural theory "lags behind" artistic production in its ability to map out or even prophesy the social impact of technological change.[12] Evidence that new media were affecting our perception of the workings of the world came as quickly as 1999, remembered by Rodowick as "the summer of digital paranoia."[13] With films such as *The Matrix*, *The Thirteenth Floor*, and *eXistenZ*, the suspicion that digital representation was qualitatively different had seeped from the viewing experience into the film texts themselves. As Rodowick observes, in these films, the world as we know it is replaced by a digital simulation, which "functions as an allegorical conflict wherein cinema struggles to reassert or define its identity in the face of a new representational technology that threatens to overwhelm it."[14] However, as he also notes, cinema has always tended to respond in this way to technologies that threaten to usurp or revolutionize it.[15] The films listed by Rodowick are of the type that Lev Manovich sees as symptomatic of cinema's return to the condition of painting. They use computer-generated imagery and effects to construct a world that is "perceptually realistic" but which has revoked analogue film's claim to mechanically record the pro-filmic world.[16] What Manovich calls "live-action footage," that is, the registration of an expressly arranged physical reality on film, now has the role of a raw material to be rearranged in postproduction.[17] Cinema moves from "kino-eye" to "kino-brush."[18] Clearly, as discussed in the previous chapter, this CGI revolution in the ontology of film and the practice of filmmaking is anathema to the ambition of Dogma 95 to resist the "film of illusion" and to capture the "instant." How are we to reconcile the use of digital video with the "kino-eye" aspirations of Dogma 95? And, along the way, can we find evidence to suggest that *Festen* exhibits Shaviro's "prophetic" function for cinema?

Given the time of its making, it was inevitable that *Festen* would be edited, distributed, consumed, and taught using digital technology. Appropriately enough for our discussion, *Festen* was the first Danish film to be issued on DVD. Crucially, however, it was not inevitable, or even intended, that it would be shot on digital. In fact, the Dogma 95 Vow of Chastity originally prescribed 35mm stock as the shooting format. However, in the time between the writing of the vow and the start of the production of *Festen*, digital video had become a feasible mode of shooting.[19] Vinterberg and his cinematographer, Anthony Dod Mantle, explain that they adopted digital video early on in the shoot primarily for financial reasons.[20] Thus it is, essentially, an accident of history that *Festen* features as a milestone in Rodowick's timeline of the digital revolution: as the earliest commercial film to "popularize" the use of the digital video camera.[21]

The 35mm Rule

The shooting format is, however, only half the story. Returning to the vow's ninth rule, we see that it states: "The film format must be Academy 35 mm." This rule has been the source of some confusion with regard to the equipment used to shoot *Festen* (and the other Dogma 95 films). Indeed, the rule's language (both in Danish and in English) is vague: it does not specify whether the films must be shot on 35mm as well as distributed in that format. This issue is clarified by the Dogme95.dk FAQs web page: "You can shoot on whatever format you want, but the final picture has to be transferred to Academy 35mm. Originally, it was a demand that the films had to be shot on Academy 35mm, but due to budgetary reasons and the good and exiting [sic] results [that] some of the directors had with Digital Video[,] [t]hey decided it was an option to shoot on DV and then transfer the films to 35mm."[22] On a purely practical level, distribution of the prints of Dogma 95 films on 35mm facilitates their screening in standard cinema venues. It implants the products of the movement firmly within existing international circuits of distribution and exhibition. Put simply, it is intended that the films be accessible to cinemagoers and critics. As the original Dogme95.dk FAQs website explains: "Dogme95 is intended to influence the current film environment."[23]

It would be churlish to suggest that this point of principle is more disingenuous than anachronistic. With a few years' hindsight, though, it raises three problems. First, an interesting thought to ponder is whether the ninth rule would have prevailed had the Dogma 95 vow been written in the age of YouTube. Would the latter have been seen as the most favorable means of distribution for a movement with democratizing ambitions? And yet it is also possible to speculate that the late-1990s "mainstreaming" of the handheld camera aesthetic paved the way for the user-generated video revolution.[24] Second, that the Dogma films' intermedial trajectory would not be unidirectional was clear; the transfer to 35mm for cinematic release was only a precursor to release on home video and (beginning in 1997) DVD. The first four Dogma 95 films, indeed, embarked on their post-theatrical journey much more prematurely than other films in Denmark did: in accordance with the funding agreement with Danmarks Radio, they were premiered on television within three months, as discussed in chapter 1. So the decision of the Dogma brethren to privilege the 35mm format in order to ensure mainstream theatrical distribution was soon overtaken by circumstance.

A third point about the 35mm rule is that it underscores the ambition of Dogma 95 to serve as a refresher course for experienced directors, rather than as a launching pad for the careers of rookie filmmakers. Were it not for this rule, making a Dogma 95 film could, in theory, be done for free, pace the costs of a consumer-quality digital video camera and generic editing software. To dictate that the film be transferred to 35mm for distribution puts the possibility of making a Dogma 95 film beyond the reach of all but those directors or producers with enough clout to attract finance. Transfer costs vary wildly, but they can run into hundreds of dollars per ten minutes of film. The Dogme95.dk FAQs admit as much: "First time directors have ultra-low budgets and therefore the transfer to Academy 35mm becomes an almost insurmountable problem." And again: "This film format rule has been one of the most criticized rules, because it is an expensive procedure and it is a bit old fashioned."[25] This last comment is telling: the attachment to 35mm is a matter not only of aesthetics but also of nostalgia.

To recapitulate, then, *Festen* emerges in the very midst of—and is shaped by—a sea change that is at once technological and cultural. One of the red threads running through this book is the extent to which *Festen* as a film text seems to be interested in the digital technology that is its condition of possibility. Dogma 95 and its first film, *Festen*, are of their time precisely because they are ambivalent about the dichotomy of analogue versus digital. Predicated as they are on capturing the "truth" of the "instant" that unfolds before the camera, the manifesto and Vow of Chastity belie a nostalgia for the index: the trace of the physical presence of the world left on the film.

Nostalgia is of course a loaded term. To unpack the concept, we need to consider not only the premillennial cultural context in which Dogma emerged—the centenary of cinema, the death of film—as outlined above. We can also acknowledge a specific strand of technological nostalgia, as diagnosed by Svetlana Boym. Introducing her book *The Future of Nostalgia*, she provides a basic definition of what she sees as a defining cultural tendency of our age: "Nostalgia (from *nostos*—return home, and *algia*—longing) is a longing for a home that no longer exists or has never existed. Nostalgia is a sentiment of loss and displacement, but it is also a romance with one's own fantasy."[26] For Boym, what is specific to nostalgia as a late-twentieth-century phenomenon, an "incurable modern condition," is that it has a "utopian dimension, only it is no longer directed toward the future."[27] Elsewhere, she writes that such nostalgia infects our relationship to technology: "That nonexistent home is akin to an ideal communal apartment where art and technology co-habited like friendly neighbours or cousins."[28] In its ambition to recapitulate a lost age of pure, raw cinema, stripped of illusionism and auteurial impositions, Dogma 95 harks back to a kind of cinema that never existed. The attachment to the 35mm format—as expressed both in the vow and by Vinterberg, above—is symptomatic of the previous decade's outbreak of mourning for analogue film among cinema scholars, critical theorists, and, not least, artists.

"It Is a Dead Medium": Dogma and Technological Nostalgia

In October 2011, the British artist Tacita Dean's installation *FILM* opened in the huge Turbine Hall at the Tate Modern Gallery, on London's South Bank. Many press reviews ran with the backstory that the installation had been shaped by Dean's shock a year before, when the processing lab Soho Film Laboratories had ceased, overnight, to develop 16mm films.[29] Clearly distressed by this threat to her life's work as a film artist, Dean herself wrote movingly about her own experience of shooting, handling, and cutting her films as physical objects, demonstrating the very real, felt, impact on practitioners of the forced obsolescence of unprofitable media:

This is why the film image is different from the digital image: it is not only emulsion versus pixels, or light versus electronics but something deeper—something to do with poetry.

Many of us are exhausted from grieving over the dismantling of analogue technologies. Digital is not better than analogue, but different. What we are asking for is co-existence: that analogue film might be allowed to remain an option for those who want it, and for the ascendency of one not to have to mean the extinguishing of the other.[30]

Dean has been able to use her privileged position as exhibitor in the Tate Turbine Hall to foster media debate about the fate of celluloid film. The book accompanying the installation attracted contributions on the importance of analogue film from some eighty artists, filmmakers, and cultural figures.[31] Ultimately, Dean argues, the fate of celluloid ought not to be left to market forces but should be brought under the aegis of national cultural policy.[32]

Dean's intervention brings home the speed with which digital production and distribution have colonized the industry. In the space of one and a half decades, the battlefront has moved. In 1995–98, the Dogma 95 brethren staged an act of resistance against the encroaching forces of illusionistic technology, ultimately exploiting the digital video camera as a weapon in the fight against mainstream cinematic convention. By 2011, filmmakers were allying with artists in a last stand against the commercial imperatives that threaten to abolish the processes and expertise essential to working with analogue film—including the 35mm format that, for Dogma 95, was still the default medium of distribution. In 2011, what seemed to be at stake for Dean and others was the craft, the feel, the look, the physical object. For Dogma 95, the stakes were the authentic, immediate access to the "real" assumed to be provided by analogue film, but which could, it transpired, be achieved in a different way in a different format.

It is also instructive to compare and contrast the respective aesthetic strategies of Dean and Dogma 95. Dean's *FILM* installation consists of an eleven-minute projection onto the back wall of the Turbine Hall. To fit the architecture of the space, the screen (and thus the camera lens and the projector) is turned ninety degrees to the vertical. Over the five months of its exhibition (from October 2011 to March 2012), the 35mm film will increasingly show signs of wear and tear. The piece thus draws the attention of visitors to the material nature of the film medium; by changing the orientation of the screen and enabling visitors to find their own viewing position within a space that in no sense resembles a cinema, it also demands reflection on conventional viewing practices. Most interesting for our discussion, the film is dominated by images that are very far from Manovich's notion that analogue film is about "live-action footage" or "the attempt to make art out of a footprint":[33] these images bear witness to Dean's manual labor as editor, to splicing, tinting, collage. As Manovich acknowledges, avant-garde filmmakers experimented with such techniques throughout the twentieth century, but on the margins of cinema: "When the avant-garde filmmakers collaged multiple images within a single frame, or painted and scratched film, or revolted against the indexical identity of cinema in other ways, they were working against 'normal' filmmaking procedures and the intended uses of film technology" (306). He goes on to point out that these aesthetic strategies later inspired the operations and interfaces of digital editing software, including cut-and-paste, painting, animation, and compositing (306–7). Thus Dean's *FILM* installation is a showcase for how celluloid can be manipulated by the artist in ways that could be replicated in digital format; it is not about a longing for a minimally mediated indexical registration of the pro-filmic world.

Conversely, the language of the Dogma 95 manifesto does betray a nostalgia for tamperproof "lens-based recordings of reality."[34] The manifesto pits itself against the winds of technological change, warning that the democratization of filmmaking will need to be countered by the avant-garde: "Today a technological storm is raging, the result of which will be the ultimate democratization of the cinema. For the first time, anyone can make movies. But the more accessible the media becomes, the more important the avant-garde. It is no accident that the phrase 'avant-garde' has military connotations. Discipline is the answer . . . we must put our films into uniform, because the individual film will be decadent by definition!" The "technological storm" is reiterated later in the manifesto: "Today a technological storm is raging of which the result is the elevation of cosmetics to God. By using new technology anyone at any time can wash the last grains of truth away in the deadly embrace of sensation." The manifesto is therefore in no sense a celebration of the new technologies emerging at the time of its writing. With the "technological storm" blow in two dangers that must be countered: the democratization of the cinema (and thus the individual, bourgeois film) and its cosmeticization. These concerns are not merely the random bugbears of a couple of Danish filmmakers. The underlying trepidation in the face of rapid technological development is very much of its time, especially in its emphasis on the danger that cosmetic "sensation" poses to "truth." If we now try to contextualize the manifesto within the broader sociocultural anxieties of the mid-1990s, we shall see that the Dogma brethren were not alone in longing for a more reliably transparent window on the new world.

The 1990s witnessed a great deal of anxiety about the relative status of film, video, and, eventually, digital images; how should the relationship to the "real" of each kind of image be understood? Writing in the early 1990s, the French philosopher Jean Baudrillard saw a qualitative difference between analogue and video.[35] The latter posed a political problem for Baudrillard, as television schedules began to foster the restaging and proliferation of "events," and the victims and participants in catastrophes found themselves caught up in their own televisual spectacle: "Photographic or cinema images still pass through the negative stage (and that of projection), whereas the TV image, the video image, digital and synthetic, are images without a negative, and hence without negativity and without reference. They are virtual and the virtual is what puts an end to all negativity, and thus to all reference to the real or to events."[36] Baudrillard's emphasis on the "negative" produced in analogue photography as a trustworthy mark of the image's relation to the "real" event chimes with the later resurgence of interest in indexicality that was engendered by the advent of the digital. The analogue image had been blessed in the twentieth century by a canon of beautifully written film-theoretical expositions of its ontology. These interventions tend to emphasize the physical (indexical) trace left by light on a photosensitive chemical surface. For André Bazin, for example, the advent of the photographic image had fulfilled the ambition of the ancients to guarantee the preservation of their dead. Bazin muses that the origins of the plastic arts lie in the desire to preserve the body: "If the plastic arts were put under psychoanalysis, the practice of embalming the dead might turn out to be a fundamental factor in their creation. The process might reveal that at the origin of painting and sculpture there lies a mummy complex."[37] For the ancient Egyptians, Bazin goes on, the corporeal bodies of the dead must be preserved at all costs; as extra insurance, terra-cotta statuettes were placed in the sarcophagi, lest the mummified bodies were destroyed or stolen. This was a Plan B, we might say, being only the "preservation of life by a representation of life" (10). Bazin goes on to show how mummification and the terra-cotta statuettes stand for two strands of art's response to the real through the ages: on the one hand, "the *duplication* of the world outside" (the mummified bodies) and, on the other, "the *expression of spiritual reality*" (the terra-cotta statuettes) (11; my emphasis). Cinema and photography, Bazin thinks, have freed the plastic arts from the first of these tasks, leading to a crisis of realism in the plastic arts in modern times (12–13). In another influential intervention, Roland Barthes, in his last book, *Camera Lucida*, published in 1980, was adamant that the same quality of objective indexicality could not be attributed to the cinema—only to still photography, in which the subject has the quality of "that-has-been" and the presence of the dead loved one, Barthes writes, "touch[es] me [with] the delayed rays of a star."[38] But for Bazin, the "impassive lens" of the cinema can capture the duration of things, such that the cinema can be described as "objectivity in time" and "change mummified."[39] In an intriguing little footnote, Bazin compares the indexical quality of photography to that of the molding of death masks: both art forms, he says, "involve a certain automatic process" and "the taking of an impression."[40] The photographic arts, then, are the inheritors of the art of the embalmer.

Such canonical approaches to the ontology of the photographic image are seductive in their insistence on the physical alchemy of light on photographic emulsion. But film theorists have begun to question how exclusive is the claim of analogue film to indexicality. Rodowick interrogates the nature of the digital image at some length in *The Virtual Life of Film*. He concludes that digital image capture may well fulfill the social function of the photograph, in that it provides a record of events in space. In fact, the digital image does this so effectively that we forget that "the digital record is a symbolic form and thus, logically, is more similar to a written description than to a visual impression."[41] This is so because, Rodowick explains, a digital camera is actually a computer whose input device is a lens.

The input data is light, which is converted to symbolic (mathematical) notation.[42] A different point of view is provided by Laura U. Marks, who argues for an understanding of the path of electrons through the device as another kind of quasi indexicality.[43] For Laura Mulvey, meanwhile, it is the changes in spectatorship wrought by the new technology that returns the stillness of the index to the cinema. Before home video and, especially, DVD, viewers were restricted to theatrical screenings. The ability to still, rewind, and view by chapter can reveal "cinema's stillness, a projected film's best-kept secret."[44] Thus, for Mulvey, the irony of the digital is that it makes possible "the frozen frame [that] restores to the moving image the heavy presence of passing time and of the mortality that Bazin and Barthes associate with the still photograph."[45]

The adoption of digital video would, then, seem to be anathema to Dogma 95, given the longing expressed in the manifesto and vow for direct access to "the truth of characters and situations" in a virginal pro-filmic space. How can one resist "the film of illusion" if what transpires before the camera is not immediately etched onto the film's surface but transcoded into a series of mathematical notations, decoded onto a computer screen as a "description" of events, and eventually transmediated to film? In an interview titled, ironically, "Denmark's DV Director," given around the time of *Festen*'s release, Vinterberg's comments on the shortcomings of digital succinctly capture precisely this paradox. On the use of video, he states:

> I am actually a bit [opposed] myself. Because it's not organic. It could sound like vanity for the film, but it is actually [true]. The digital thing makes it somewhat cold. Which happens to be okay for this film, because it's the cold registration of something very troubling. But it doesn't create life to shoot on video. Not at all.

It is a dead medium. Completely. And to be honest, I would have preferred to shoot this on Academy 35.[46]

Vinterberg's use of the word "organic" here is telling, for it unconsciously echoes a neologism that Manovich reports was common parlance among CGI specialists in Hollywood in 1996: human actors were referred to as "organics" or, alternatively, "soft fuzzies."[47] Manovich in the course of his discussion of how digital technology is revolutionizing the very nature of cinema adroitly turns the notion of analogue film as "organic" and alive on its head:

> Yet behind even the most stylized cinematic images, we can discern the bluntness, sterility, and banality of early nineteenth-century photographs. No matter how complex its stylistic innovations, the cinema has found its base in these deposits of reality, these samples obtained by a methodical and prosaic process. Cinema emerged out of the same impulse that engendered naturalism, court stenography and wax museums. Cinema is the art of the index; it is an attempt to make art out of a footprint.[48]

Little wonder that the late 1990s saw a crisis of representation in the cinema: was analogue film a record of organic life moving busily in the pro-filmic world—or was it a waxwork? Was analogue film a medium in its own right, with sole prerogative over the nomenclature "cinema"—or was it, as Manovich would have it, a temporary stage in the history of artistic representation? Is digital video, as Vinterberg would have it, a "dead medium"? Is film, too, all but dead, partly thanks to the pioneering use of digital video in *Festen*?

Steven Shaviro has called for an end to such nostalgic wallowing in the slow disappearance of a medium. Shaviro insists that "such responses [to the new media regime] are inadequate. They are too wrapped up in their own melancholic sense of loss to grasp the emergence of new relations of production, and of new media forms. They miss the aesthetic poignancy of post-cinematic media."[49] Svetlana Boym's work, too, offers an optimistic antidote to the culture of mourning the passing of celluloid: her "off-modern manifesto." She reminds us that all technology is predicated on machines and interfaces that can and do break down, behave unpredictably, and thus offer opportunities for the generation of unexpected texts, images, and objects. Contemplating the blurred images wrenched from her malfunctioning printer, she realizes the potential of the error: "Erring traces unexpected connections between different forms of knowledge, art, and technology, beyond the prescribed interactivities of specific technological media; makes new flexible cognitive maps based on aesthetic knowledge and ahead of software calculations."[50] We could see *Festen*'s adoption of digital video in this light: as a pragmatically motivated and productive error. While Vinterberg and Dod Mantle, as artists and practitioners, feel nostalgia for Academy 35, they gamely wrangle with the unfamiliar technological objects that will drag their art into the future, discovering their potential to create "aesthetic poignancy."

Conclusion

As the first commercial feature film to be shot on digital video, *Festen* has become ineluctably associated with the digital revolution of the turn of the millennium. However, as we have seen in this chapter, Dogma 95 can and should be regarded as a reaction against the contemporary emergence of CGI and the increasing dominance of digitally facilitated "cosmetics" in filmmaking. Just as the Dogma 95 manifesto self-consciously inserted itself as a movement into cinema history, so too can it be seen as a response to a broader culture of "endism" in cinema at a time when the film medium was threatened by emerging technologies and by the physical disintegration of the century's film heritage. In its commitment to privileging the "truth" of the "instant," and in its original insistence on the use of the 35mm format, Dogma 95 arguably exhibits a nostalgia for film's alleged ability to fix an indexical trace of the moments it records. This nostalgia is also in evidence in the statements of the director and cinematographer on their adoption of digital video as a shooting format. This is a different dynamic from more recent expressions of nostalgia for analogue film, which emphasize its tactile qualities as an art form.

In part 2 of this book, we now turn our attention to precisely this ambivalence between the analogue and the digital, a productive tension engendered by the principles of Dogma 95 itself as well as the historical, cultural, and technological context in which *Festen* was made. We shall see that the film's technical specifications result in an exquisite interest in the bodies—dead and very much alive—that are at the heart of the film's disturbing narrative. This produces a kind of post-filmic indexicality, in which the guarantee of the indexical trace is replaced by bodily presence, texture, and an emphasis on the senses.

PART TWO

Festen's Bodies

4.1　A shell-shocked guest after Helene has read the letter and Helge, Else, and Christian have exited the dining room

4

The Handheld Camera

People say the Dogme concept now needs five people to work the camera—one to hold it and the other four to shake him or her.
—Ingmar Bergman, "Pure Kamikaze"

*H*elene has read out Linda's letter to the assembled company. The father, enraged, has acknowledged, indeed, justified, his abuse of his children: "It was all you were good for." Father and mother troop out of the dining room, shell-shocked, defeated. As Christian himself gets unsteadily to his feet and makes to leave, the camera veers drunkenly as it gets up with him and tries to right itself, finding a position in line with the door out to the next room, just as Christian staggers through. The camera sits still now, doesn't follow Christian through the door. We watch as he crosses the light room beyond, steadies himself on the doorframe to the next room, and disappears from view. Close to the camera, though, on the right-hand side of the screen, is a woman, youngish, dark-haired, an anonymous guest. Throughout Christian's slow exit from the scene of battle she is trapped there, in semi-profile. As Christian exits, she turns her head to the right to watch him leave, then turns back to look straight ahead of her, raising her eyebrows to a companion in a gesture of shocked complicity. The indefatigable Helmut suggests a spot of dancing and coffee. The woman's eyes flicker for a moment. Her face seems to be trying to resolve itself into an expression. But how is she to react? The shot lingers for a couple of seconds more. She seems uncomfortable, so close to the camera.

"Sticking It to the Steadicam Generation"

Cameraman scrambling to follow actor, camera infringing on the personal space of an extra, the extra unsure how to react to the revelations she has just heard: all clichés of the Dogma 95 aesthetic that *Festen* established and which seem to have garnered Ingmar Bergman's mirth. The "shaky camera" look has become popularly synonymous with a certain kind of late-1990s low-budget filmmaking; frantic camerawork is, after all, the most immediately visible symptom of the Dogma 95 influence. To appreciate the contemporary reception of this quite distinctive "look," one only has to turn to an early, and somewhat curmudgeonly, review in *Sight and Sound*:

> From neo-realism to *cinéma vérité*, film history has reliably proved authenticity is a chimerical goal. Sooner or later, the impression of raw immediacy congeals and stands exposed as a style like any other. Initially, and for a long stretch, *Festen* seems to confirm one's scepticism. Vinterberg sticks it to the steadicam generation with a jumble of impeccably ugly shots, ranging from the bleached-out and watery to the muddily indecipherable (it doesn't help that it has been transferred from video). . . .

If a transparency of means is the true object of *Festen*, then it bombs out miserably. Peering as one must through a perpetual celluloid haze and juggled about by the off-kilter, fun-house framing, one is made highly conscious of the thick material contrivance of the image.[1]

Despite the reviewer's jaded air, he has clearly been rattled by *Festen*'s cinematography. The effect, it seems, is produced by a *combination* of the use of handheld camera and the transfer from video to film. Why is this mix so potent? *Festen*'s handheld camera was anticipated in Lars von Trier's *Breaking the Waves* (1996), which was nonetheless shot on 35mm (and transferred to video and back again, giving a murky look). It was most notoriously succeeded by *The Blair Witch Project*'s use, in 1999, of portable video cameras operated by the actors themselves, and by Mike Figgis's experimental *Timecode* (2000), which juxtaposes four on-screen frames of simultaneous action. Even among this very small selection of popularly and critically acclaimed films from the four-year period around the making of *Festen*, we see that "handheld" is not synonymous with "digital." Herein lies *Festen*'s power to move the viewer (and the reviewer), literally and metaphorically.

Handheld, after all, was hardly new. Starting in the 1920s, the Bolex 16mm camera was in use for newsreel production, and by the Second World War it was commonplace to use Arriflex and similar handheld cameras in the field for documentary and reportage.[2] Direct cinema, cinéma vérité, and free cinema made use of the possibilities afforded by mobile 16mm cameras and other formats from the 1950s on, as did avant-garde film artists. The handheld camera and jump cuts of Jean-Luc Godard's *À bout de souffle* (Breathless; 1960) became the calling cards of the French New Wave, but Godard was also an "early adopter" of video (the Sony Portapak) as a mobile shooting format.³ By 1992, footage from the 1989 Romanian revolution shot on camcorders had already been co-opted into documentary by Harun Farocki, whose seminal project *Videogramme einer Revolution* (Videograms of a Revolution; 1992) presaged how individual citizens armed with digital camcorders could record, and thus shape, history.⁴

Neither should we overromanticize the handheld camera as a revolutionary means of allowing an otherwise immobilized camera operator to move toward the action. Dziga Vertov's *Man with a Movie Camera* reveals just how peripatetic a man with a camera on a tripod could be, even on the streets of Moscow in 1929. More recently, the widespread use of the Steadicam mount and counterweight has afforded flexibility and motility to operators of a range of cameras (Peter Matthews's "steadicam generation"), albeit the harness, as the trademarked name suggests, is specifically designed to mitigate against camera shake.

What was new in the *Festen* era was the size and weight of the latest cameras. It is poignant to note here that the first portable video cameras had been adopted in the mid-1970s by feminist artists because of the cameras' *weightiness* and concomitant potential for empowerment. The artist Shigeko Kubota, for example, is recorded as declaring that she enjoyed traveling the world independently with her Portapak "tear[ing] down [her] shoulder, backbone and waist."⁵ Twenty years later, it is not the weight of the digital video camera that cripples Anthony Dod Mantle, but the acrobatics he is able to perform while holding it: "crawling around like a dog," in Vinterberg's words.⁶ Interviews around the time of *Festen*'s release hint at the novelty of such equipment even for specialist journalists, as director and cinematographer repeatedly use props—glasses, mugs, tape recorders—to illustrate just how small the cameras were. Dod Mantle explains his choice this way:

Well, there were Panasonics and Canons around, but for me the only camera that really sat in my hand and made me feel "This is a weapon" was the Sony PC7–E, a first-generation consumer camera, single-chip, *about twice the size of this glass.* . . . What I gained was agility, mobility, accessibility—what I call the "emotional movement" of these small cameras, as opposed to the more premeditated movement you have to do when you have a heavy film camera on the shoulder.[7]

The technological conditions under which *Festen* was shot are thus very historically specific. If the technology was new, though, the principles, or the film-historical heritage, that informed its use were anything but. Against this background, we now turn to look at a more specific line of descent that informs Dogma 95's insistence on handheld cameras.

Faces and *Faces*

In an interview in 2007, Vinterberg spoke in some detail on his fondness for shooting handheld. He had originally wanted to shoot his previous film, *De største helte* (The Greatest Heroes; 1996), in low-budget style, after his positive experience with handheld cameras at film school:

> And I remember . . . I'm jumping back now to my junior year film, *Brudevalsen* [The Bridal Waltz] it was called; we had to make a fifteen-minute film in a very short space of time. At the film school. So I roped in the photographer who did tai chi and could hold a camera still, and I threw all the camera equipment away and said, we're going to do this film handheld. And

nobody had done that here in Denmark before. And that's the one that von Trier saw. It was that film he saw when he asked me to do Dogma.[8]

Where did this precocious idea come from? Vinterberg (like von Trier and other directors and actors of their generation in Denmark) is often quoted as citing the American independent director John Cassavetes as an influence on his style and on his understanding of the purpose of cinema.[9] Though he stops short of analyzing *Festen*, film scholar Angelos Koutsourakis has gone so far as to claim that "Cassavetes and Dogme share the same ambition, namely to bring cinema back to life by changing our understanding and our perception of the medium as something more than a means of articulating a discernible diegetic world," and, further, that they share "an oppositional realist form that blurs the boundaries between being and performing."[10] Given this at least circumstantial evidence of the influence of his work on the Dogma 95 founders, the work of Cassavetes is a very good place to start in order to try to grasp the practical and film-philosophical implications of the use of the handheld camera in *Festen*.

Let's consider the face of our anonymous female guest, as shown at the start of this chapter, caught by the doorway as the hero staggers out. Her discomfiture seems typical of the trial that the extras at the dinner table were forced to undergo as the evening's speeches played out. It is known that the dinner guests were less than thoroughly briefed, as Vinterberg explains:

> Well, we didn't tell the extras that the film was about child abuse, or that Christian was going to make that kind of speech. . . . So they were all there at the location for fourteen days, becoming a family. All huge fans of the father, Henning Moritzen, who's done forty films in Denmark as the good guy.

> Suddenly this guy Christian stands up and reveals all. And it was interesting, because nothing really happened! Quite a "true" moment actually. People couldn't really deal with it—so they just kept . . . talking.[11]

Vinterberg goes on to reminisce that the reactions of the extras were so subtle as to render much of the footage unusable. Paprika Steen, who plays Helene in the film, astutely comments that reactions to such revelations or crises tend to be culturally specific: it is socially mandated in Denmark to underreact, rather than overreact.[12] The moment of revelation to an unbriefed crowd opens up a space in which the people in the room—neither entirely as actors or characters—come to terms with a genuine, collective shock. After each successive speech and its revelations, the cameras move from person to person, collecting reactions as they play out over faces. Significant here is that cameras were assigned to actors during this scene, so that a range of responses could be captured, more or less at random, from *within* the "audience," while the speech unfolded its revelations.[13]

This episode in *Festen* is a relatively undramatic counterpoint to von Trier's deliberate and sustained blurring of the boundaries between character and actor in his Dogma film, *The Idiots*.[14] Nevertheless, it is an excellent illustration of a strategy of controlled improvisation that seems to have made its way from direct cinema to Dogma 95. Todd Berliner expresses the potential of this approach very clearly: "Conspicuous improvisation tends to call attention to the artistic process because it encourages audiences to notice not just the behavior of the characters but also that of the actors playing them. But improvisation is not solely the activity of professional performers; when real people speak, most of the time they are improvising. Hence actors who appear to be improvising also appear to behave more like real people."[15] Our time with the guest [in fig. 4.1] though,

4.2   A guest reacts to Christian's revelations

is special in its sustained interest in her confused but self-contained response. We might at first glance remark that this unadorned shot is classic Cassavetes, whose self-declared philosophy as a director was that "audiences go to the cinema to see people: they only empathize with people and not with technical virtuosity."[16] However, scholarly interest in Cassavetes has recently probed beyond his self-declared lack of interest in film technique to reveal a methodology that is not merely about capturing improvised interactions between characters. George Kouvaros, for example, argues that such lingering shots ("dead time," as he calls them) "test the limits of character by exploring the pressures and relations which surround the performance of

4.3   The last shot of the film. Christian's inscrutable face in lingering close-up

the drama but are usually excluded from the final print."[17] In other words, these lingering face shots are interrogations of the nature of acting, of the tension between actor and character. Another shot in *Festen* that we might fruitfully consider from this point of view is the very last one. Christian's father has left the breakfast room, and the camera holds Christian's face in extreme close-up for a full fourteen seconds as he (presumably) watches his father walk away and, at length, glances down toward the table.

In both of these cases (and in many more instances throughout *Festen*), the viewer is forced into an uncomfortably long and discomfitingly close engagement with the face on-screen as expressions or "micro-movements" flicker across it.[18] This is a clear example of the creation of the "affective contract" with the spectator that we discussed in chapter 1, a meeting that takes place in space that is at once concrete and virtual, sensory and metaphorical.[19] Indeed, for Gilles Deleuze, "the affection-image is the close-up, and the close-up is the face."[20] Face-to-face, we can find ourselves in an intense encounter with this body, this moment detached from the narrative; our cocreation of this affective event fulfills the Dogma 95 exhortation to force the truth out of characters and situations.

Vinterberg has attributed his tendency to show who is seeing, rather than what is seen, to the influence of Andrei Tarkovsky's *Сталкер* (Stalker; 1979), in which a trio ride on a trolley into a forbidden area, through a landscape that is never seen by the viewer: "I remember that trip on the trolley as something that opened my world of cinematography. . . . I believe that the audience remember that trip with the trolley as if they had been watching a huge landscape themselves, but they've only seen faces experiencing it."[21] But this closing shot of Christian's face bears further scrutiny, I think, and who better to help than Cassavetes, the director responsible for the five-hour handheld epic *Faces* (1968). The whole weight of the film rests on Christian's reaction to a "battle well fought," as his departing father puts it. In retrospect, then, this shot has what we might call a metafictive function. This effect is intensified by the perceptible increase in ambient sound levels throughout the shot. The sound is thus defamiliarized as it builds to a sudden cut to blackness and the end titles. The film is flagging its own imminent expiry by electronic means, just as it announced its arrival with the insistent trill of the mobile telephone. To quote Kouvaros on Cassavetes again:

> During such moments we are presented with "dead time": an expenditure of energy and film stock that in narrative terms

contributes little to our understanding of the characters, their motivations or problems. It is at this juncture, when, to borrow a phrase used by Antonioni, "everything already seems to have been said," that what critics bluntly dismiss as evidence of Cassavetes's penchant for improvisation reveals itself as a deliberate attempt to open the performance of character up to resonances, questions and points of view which cannot be answered or contained by the narrative.[22]

In digital cinema there can, of course, be no question of wastage of film stock; as Peter Schepelern remarks, Dogma filmmakers frequently shot many times more material than they needed, as well as improvisations, without any fear of burning money.[23] The point about "expenditure of energy" remains, though, and this idea opens out into a second aspect of Dogma 95 strategy that Cassavetes's practice can illuminate. This is the creation of the event.

Taking Place

Getting indecently close to the actors' faces is one use for a very small, mobile camera. But the third rule of the Dogma 95 Vow of Chastity encourages more mobility. To recap:

3 The camera must be handheld. Any movement or immobility attainable in the hand is permitted. (The film must not *take place* where the camera is standing; shooting must take place where the film *takes place*.) (Emphasis added.)

This is reminiscent of Cassavetes's own descriptions of his practice. On the making of his film *Shadows*, he says:

> So we not only improvised in terms of the words, but we improvised in terms of motions. The cameraman also improvised. He had to follow the artists so that the actors could move when and wherever they pleased. . . . In fact, when you try it, you find that natural movement is easier to follow than rehearsed movement since it has a natural rhythm. Whereas when they rehearse something according to a technical mark, they begin to be jerky and unnatural, and no matter how talented they are, the camera has a difficult time following them.[24]

The theory is clear: the camera physically follows the action. But is that the whole story? Let's consider for a moment the comment of the *Sight and Sound* reviewer, who has misgivings that, in *Festen*, "half the commotion is dictated by the need to justify the camerawork, instead of the other way round."[25] This is meant as a criticism, but it also reveals something about how the film, to take literally the vow's formulation, "takes place." Cassavetes's brand of direct cinema—with its handheld cameras, found locations, naturalistic (if not improvised) dialogue, and recurring band of actors—is not just about setting an event in motion, following it, and passively capturing it. Neither, we might say, is that the philosophy of Dogma 95. Rather, the interaction of camera and actor(s)—and viewer—actually produces the event. Kouvaros's description of the premises of direct cinema could also apply to Dogma 95: "Contrary to the way it is often positioned, Direct Cinema does not involve an attempt to reproduce life or capture a reality that would pre-exist it, but is based rather on the productive and affective relation between the cinema and the events, stories and fictions it constructs."[26] Discussing *Faces*, he goes on to describe the role of the camera as a "catalyst for initiating and provoking the performances" and as a quasi character that "engages with, and is affected by, the material it simultaneously records and constructs."[27] This is a very seductive way to think about the camera's activity in *Festen*. Two sequences should suffice to demonstrate how the camera co-conspires to make the action "take place" in quite different ways.

The first scene occurs directly after Christian's exit from the dining room, as described at the start of this chapter. As the shot opens, the quality of light has deteriorated sharply despite what appears to be a chandelier overhead, and a hand reaches out to light a candle directly in front of the camera. This gesture could be interpreted as an impudent reference to the ban on sources of artificial light; it also has the effect of delimiting the space for what will occur, setting place in motion. A waltz is played on the piano, and people dance. The camera whirls out onto the dance floor, at knee height. It finds Gbatokai and Helene entwined under the chandelier and starts to waltz dizzily with them.

It is reasonably obvious that in this shot the actors are actually holding the camera themselves, at arms' length.[28] This has several effects. It draws attention to the handheld camera in yet another new way, refreshing the film's (and the spectator's) interest in its technology here, close to the end of the film. The camera is set in motion by the couple's dancing, and it thus imbues their waltz with emotion, triggering an affective response from the viewer, who also feels as though he or she is moving and being moved.[29] The camera does not merely follow and film the dance; it is part of the dance and constructs not just its motion but also its emotion. We might also observe that it is crucial that Gbatokai, the outsider who had been the target of racist abuse earlier in the evening, is here incorporated into the intimate space of the film, indeed, collaborating in its creation.

An earlier and quite different sequence, sixteen minutes into the film, places the camera in the hotel room of Michael and his wife,

4.4   The camera is held at arm's length by the dancers

Mette, as he tries to find his dress shoes and they start fighting. The scene is characterized by an energetic mix of pans from face to face and jump cuts. Throughout, in the confined space, the camera follows the gestures of the couple demonstratively. For example, it follows Mette's searching hands into the family's bags. It follows Michael's gaze ostentatiously down to his white sports socks when he mentions his badly shod feet. It also conspires in an improvised moment from Thomas Bo Larsen as Michael, as he takes a slurp of water from his glass and slams it down on the table to ready himself for the coming fight.[30] The camera could thus be said to provide the visual punctuation (or deixis) necessary in such a frantic and comedic scene. The tiny bedroom thus becomes a space that is both tactile and three-dimensional (Mette's rummaging) and subjective (the jump cuts occasioned by the incoherent screams of fury and bile). This scene is crosscut with ongoing action in two other bedrooms, as we shall see later in chapter 8—Pia is chatting with Christian and taking a bath, while Helene and Lars are preparing her bedroom.

But Michael and Mette's scene continues to "take place" with a shift in gear by the camera. After their argument, they sit down, each on their respective single beds. The camera crouches, waiting, like Michael does, for Mette's permission to pounce—there is an obvious shift in power toward Mette in this erotically charged context. When she gives the word, Michael moves toward her; there is a cut to elsewhere in the hotel, and upon our return to their bedroom, we watch from a high angle as they engage in vigorous sexual intercourse. Among Vinterberg's postproduction confessions is that a camera was tied to a microphone boom in order to achieve a particular smooth, swooping motion from high angle to low. This distinctive shot lasts approximately ten seconds and effectively transforms the schizophrenic space of the room to continuous space. We cut from high-angle surveillance of Michael and Mette having sex to Michael's postcoital humming in the shower. The camera makes a circular swooping motion around the room, continuing its arc to study Mette's inscrutable expression in a sideways-on close-up, lying beside her as she lies on the tangled sheets. This distinctive camera movement, quite different from what has gone before, flags the shift from our distanced, aerial surveillance of an act of bodily intimacy, back to a relationship of affective intimacy within reach of Mette's peri-personal space. It is as though the act of penetration we witness from a distance stands for the bodily and emotional intimacy we almost (but never quite) achieve at other times with the bodies on-screen.

Lastly, we can also note another, more banal and generalized, quality afforded to the film by the handheld camera: the sense of a crowded, milling space. People's heads are always getting in the way of a shot. For example, as Helge opens the door to the parlor to receive the guests, we first see him from behind a guest's shoulder, a blurry outline of a guest's head obscuring his grand entrance. During the pre-party singing, Pia asks to borrow Christian's shower. She is obscured during the conversation by another guest's blurry head swaying in front of the camera. Later, as Michael returns from his assault on Michelle, there is an incongruous close-up of lips as out-of-focus figures walk past in the background. Most poignantly, the lingering close-ups of Helene as she reads her sister's suicide note at the film's climax features some wavy hair swinging in and out of shot on the right-hand side of the screen.

Such invasions of the camera's peri-personal space are also typical of Cassavetes's style, in *Faces*, for example. They confirm that the camera is genuinely embedded within the collective event it is recording and thus caught up in its ongoing creation. Such extreme proximity to unexpected facial profiles and heads also invests the film with a thoroughgoing sense of fleshliness. The camera is embedded, and by extension embodied, in a space full of human life. The result, to quote Berliner, is "a realism created not by concealing one's art but by revealing the similarity between the act of creating art and the act of living."[31]

Conclusion

The handheld camera is the technological novelty most popularly associated with *Festen*, precisely because the most distinctive aspect of *Festen*'s style is its "shaky" camera. The use of handheld cameras

4.5   A guest's profile intrudes into the frame

has a heritage almost as old as cinema itself and is thus emblematic of a range of genres spanning documentary and art house cinema. Both Vinterberg and von Trier had experimented previously with handheld shooting, inspired in particular by the work of Cassavetes. Indeed, the vow's insistence on the use of a handheld camera can be distinguished from Vinterberg and Dod Mantle's later decision to adopt a particular kind of handheld camera, that is, the latest generation of digital camcorder. Nevertheless, the handheld cameras used to shoot *Festen* facilitate relationships between space, body, camera, image, and viewer that conjure into existence particularly intense events. Sequences such as Michael and Mette's fight scene, or extended close-ups of faces, can be understood to be informed by the techniques of Cassavetes and others. However, they are also an important locus for the generation of the "affective contract" with the viewer, which is integral to Dogma 95's commitment to forcing the truth out of characters and situations and which is also implicit in Dod Mantle's reference to the "emotional movement" of his camera. We now turn to examine the space in which the film, more broadly speaking, "takes place": the space of the hotel.

5
The Hotel

Film—the screen of light—is read as it is traversed and is readable inasmuch as it is traversable. As we go through it, it goes through us. The "visitor" is the subject of this practice: a passage through light spaces.
—Giuliana Bruno, *Atlas of Emotion*

A *cawing bird swoops over the treetops across the dawn sky. Calmly, with just the merest of quivering reminding us that it is still handheld, the camera presents to us the most classically beautiful shot of the film: the manor house in the misty dawn light. For the first time, the colors and architectural styles of the house are seen as a harmonious whole, reflected in the perfectly still water of the lake. One curling reed cuts through the foreground. Cut to the table being laid for breakfast in the sunshine.*

We need only witness the acknowledgment in *Festen*'s end credits—"we are profoundly, unreservedly grateful to Skjoldenæsholm Hotel and Conference Center and to Susanne Bruun de Neergaard"

5.1   The hotel at dawn

—to be reminded of the deep debt that every Dogma 95 film owes to its location. The first Dogma rule, it will be remembered, reads as follows: "Shooting must be done on location. Props and sets must not be brought in." The pragmatic filmmaker, then, will settle on a location that provides access to a wide range of potential props, as well as the right kind of space for the story to unfold. Extratextual considerations will tend to prevail: What can the production afford? Where will the actors and crew sleep? A set of pragmatic choices and compromises thus imposes on the production a delimited space and a finite set of available props and sets. The ways in which these material conditions are put into service during the filmmaking process inflect the film text in often fascinating ways. For example, Ellen Rees has observed that the first three Danish Dogma 95 films unfold within and around large family homes, the story in each case centering on a resistance to, or a coming-to-terms with, the patriarchal power invested in the place.[1] In this light, we can see that the first rule, by imposing the necessity of a complex, flexible, and well-equipped location for the shoot, mandates narratives that explore the use of space and the play of power and memory in space.

This chapter explores how the material environment of the hotel shapes the narrative in *Festen* and how the space of the hotel is mediated in the film text by dint of the Dogma 95 regulations. This discussion of the hotel space acts as a precursor to chapter 6, where consideration is given to how the restrictions on importing props and sets can also be seen to draw attention to the manipulation of objects in the physical environment as focal points and objects of memory.

Skjoldenæsholm: Space, Time, Architecture

The Skjoldenæsholm Hotel and Conference Center is located near the town of Ringsted, southwest of Copenhagen. The Danish manor house hotel is a cultural phenomenon in its own right. Skjoldenæsholm has a history typical of such a house: a main building constructed in neoclassical style in the eighteenth century, on the site of a fourteenth-century royal residence, and eventually restored in the late twentieth century for mixed commercial use for corporate and private conferencing, fine dining, and recreation.[2] Skjoldenæsholm is of sufficient historical significance to feature as an entry both in the *Danish National Encyclopedia* (*Den Store Danske Encyklopædi*) and in the

Danish Ministry of Culture's online project *1001 Stories of Denmark*.³ Its significance stems from its location on medieval royal land, its architectural composition, and the artifacts in possession of the Bruun de Neergaard family. The building is thus part of Denmark's national architectural heritage, functioning as ancient family seat, as museum, and as hotel.

The historic hotel and the national museum have much in common as spaces. They both easily fall under the category of *heterotopia* proposed by Michel Foucault: real spaces a little outside society but integral to it, often spaces of deviation or crisis, such as the cemetery, the library, or the hospital or, indeed, the museum and the hotel.⁴ Time flows through heterotopias in distinctive ways, thinks Foucault, and he proposes the term *heterochronies* to flag how heterotopias process time in ways that are integral to their respective functions. The museum, for example, is a storehouse of history, an accumulation of time. Foucault does not explain the heterochrony of the hotel. However, a few moments' thought suggests that the space-time of the historic hotel is complex and fascinating.

The fabric of Skjoldenæsholm incorporates expressions of a number of eras: a half-timbered wing dating from 1662, the neoclassical main building of 1766, and the architectural concessions to modern habits (en suite bathrooms, for example). Skjoldenæsholm's publicity materials emphasize the idea of the location as a palimpsest of the traces of different eras. Especially notable is the discussion of ongoing renovations of the adjoining parklands, under which the paths and beds of a baroque garden are said to be buried. Skjoldenæsholm offers "the atmosphere of past times combined with modern comforts" to the discerning Danish traveler.⁵ Nevertheless, the workaday temporal rhythms and cycles of less historically rooted hotels prevail. By definition, the hotel houses a transitory population. The traces of each guest must be erased—through the invisible labors of housekeeping staff—before the next arrives. Every check-in starts a countdown of rented moments, priced per night, according to square footage, quality of decor, and amenities. In this sense, for all its authentic historical resonance, Skjoldenæsholm is a classic example of the French anthropologist Marc Augé's supermodern "non-place," a clinical space through which humans pass, but which is outside the social networks of memory and community that weave individual lives together.[6]

The hotel is thus a curious heterochrony, and the scenario sketched out in *Festen* makes it more so. Helge's party guests are not really guests at all, but family and friends. They check in to hotel rooms for which they have not paid, for the single overnight stay delineated by the film's dramaturgical unity. The party guests are thus gathering in a "non-place," but one that is also a site of familial memory and history. Their needs are met by a small army of staff who move through and work in service spaces usually invisible to the guests: the kitchen, the corridors, the wine cellar. The kitchen staff regulate the pace and timing of serving food and clearing up via an intercom system, which incidentally, but crucially for the plot, allows them to listen in on goings-on in the dining room. The tension between private and public space that is inherent in any hotel is thus especially acute—and productively so—in *Festen*. The camerawork conspires to cocreate and exploit this spatiotemporal ambiguity and liminality.

Building on Sergei Eisenstein's essay "Montage and Architecture," cultural theorist Giuliana Bruno traces the historical connections between the development of architectural tradition and film spectatorship. Sitting in the cinema or on the sofa, the film viewer's ability to grasp the continuities and discontinuities of space and time is analogous to his or her apprehension of spaces through which he or she might, at other times, move: "The (im)mobile spectator moves across an imaginary path, traversing multiple sites and times. Her fictional navigation connects distant moments and far-apart places. Film inherits the possibility of such a spectatorial voyage from the architectural field, for the person who wanders through a building or a site also absorbs and connects visual spaces."[7] Of course, this movement is illusory, for as Lev Manovich reminds us, the viewing regime of cinema is predicated on "institutionalized immobility."[8] The spectator sits still, usually in the dark, in a physical space, and is led through a virtual space elsewhere. But even this convention has its own genealogy. Manovich sees its origins in Renaissance painting, which, unlike earlier frescoes and mosaics, were separate from the wall or room in which they were exhibited. To appreciate a fresco, the spectator can move around in the architectural space on which it is painted. A post-Renaissance painting, in contrast, "presents a virtual space that is clearly distinct from the physical space where the painting and spectator are located."[9]

Bruno thinks that cinema adapted the particular "ways of seeing" developed by the eighteenth-century picturesque movement in art, landscape, and architecture.[10] For example, the baroque garden now buried beneath the parkland around Skjoldenæsholm would have invited the spectator-as-perambulator to experience its minutely planned beauty as moving images, the perspective shifting with the body of the walker in the garden. Incidentally, at the time of writing, Skjoldenæsholm's website describes ongoing renovations in the parkland that reinstate a line of vision in either direction from the stream on the grounds: the prospective guest will be assured the picturesque experience of standing in the parkland with a "beautiful view" of manor house, waterfall, and lake.[11] The camera in *Festen* does not, though, take advantage of this particular vista: its concern is not to emphasize the fine geometry of the site (pace the exterior shot discussed at the beginning of this chapter) but to move the spectator in other ways.

Indeed, Bruno emphasizes that just as the picturesque required the spectator to move, imaginatively or physically, through space, cinema moves the spectator through "unexpected paths of exploration."[12] This is of course not just about camerawork. Editing or montage is crucial to the spectator's experience of film, and it echoes the human interaction with the physical environment: "Like film, architecture—apparently static—is shaped by the montage of spectatorial movements."[13] We now explore the geometries of, and perspectives on, the hotel that *Festen* opens up to us.

Thresholds and Mirrors

How does *Festen* move the spectator through the space of the hotel, and how does the architecture of the hotel space inform the spectator's apprehension of the world of the film? Posing the question in this way recognizes the spatial integrity imposed by the exhortation to shoot on location, without accusing the filmmakers of the sin of fomenting an aesthetic strategy. Nevertheless, certain patterns can be observed.

First, there is a tension between the harmonious symmetry of the neoclassical architecture and the camerawork. Put simply, the lines of the house are askew throughout the film. Moldings of doorways, balustrades, and other interior lines are almost always filmed at an angle. At the macro level, the facade of the main building receives the same treatment. Our first view of the frontage of the hotel is provided by a camera crouched behind a gate, thick with rust, as Michael's car screeches into the car lot. We pan swiftly round to watch, still from a low angle beside the stone gatepost, as the car comes to a halt in front of the manor house, and the brothers get out of the car and walk toward the main entrance. The neoclassical facade with its even rows of windows and triangular tympanum with clock is canted slightly leftward, and the top edge of the picture cuts through the pediment. Toward the end of the film, a similar effect is produced as morning approaches and Christian saves his father from Michael's wrath. The manor, light blazing from all its windows, can be seen in the background as Christian kneels down to inspect his father's condition. The camera, and thus the house, tilts sympathetically as Christian bows over his father's prostrate form.

A second tension can be observed between the handheld camera's propensity to mingle at ground level and its tendency to appropriate the vertical axis afforded by the high ceilings inside the manor house. The camera frequently takes up a kind of closed-circuit-television's-eye view, both in corridors and in the dining room during and after dinner. A sustained example starts thirteen minutes in, with an initially indistinguishable light pattern on-screen. After a few seconds the blur resolves into a corridor lit by a modernist Poul Henningsen lamp, with light flooding in at the end of the corridor. Helene is explaining to the receptionist, Lars, that she has been given her dead sister's bedroom. When the pair enters the room, the camera is lurking in a corner at ceiling height opposite the door, observing pale green walls with white paneling, a four-poster bed, and assorted items of furniture covered with white sheets. These angles are legally attainable by the canny camera operator who might, for example, take advantage of a well-placed piece of furniture to climb on. Nevertheless, the interest in verticality led to one "sin," already mentioned in the previous chapter: the smooth, swooping motion from high angle to low as Mette lies on her bed, achieved by attaching the camera to a microphone boom.

The interest in verticality also has more complex manifestations. This is established from our first entry into the house. Our first view of the interior is from a landing overlooking the entrance hall. The

5.2   Christian and Helene on the landing

door opens, letting in a shaft of sunlight through which the brothers step, preceded by their shadows on the doormat and flagstone floor. They bound up the stairs. A series of shot–reverse shots document the conversation between the brothers and the harried Lars behind the reception desk. Again, the canted effect of the doorway behind Michael is marked. A remarkable sequence early on makes use of the vertical space of the main staircase. The camera, apparently moving upstairs itself, behind a balustrade with oblong perforations, tracks Christian making his way down the sunlit staircase. Helene runs upstairs to hug Christian on the landing, and the camera ducks up over the banister to witness this.

THE HOTEL   99

5.3 Christian strides through the hallway, his back toward the dining room

The extraordinary duck-egg blue architecture of the entrance hall and stairway is again exploited much later, as Christian strides back to the dining room after he is first ejected. The camera moves in front of Christian at knee height through the hall, looking upward to his torso and head, as he walks under the landing above, his head following the line of the overhanging staircase, sunlight still streaming through the windows higher up. We crosscut to the dining room, where Helge's mother is warbling a cappella a song about the peace of the forest. And then we cut back to Christian, again from knee height, striding through the public rooms back toward the dining room and then, discordantly, from above, throwing open the successive sets of double doors.

A third tension between the architectural characteristics of the house and the camera's exploration of it consists in a reluctance to reveal its rooms as *connected*, at least in a way that is easily comprehensible to the viewer. Put differently, the camera has boundary issues. It is clear that the ground floor of the manor consists of an interconnected series of public rooms and that the kitchen is in the basement, reached via a staircase. But even a key sequence for our understanding of the space, in which the public rooms are traversed in sequence by Michael, presents the connected rooms as disconnected. Before the party starts, Helge enters Michael's bedroom, where he is still getting dressed, and orders his son to come to a meeting in the parlor in five minutes. Michael's trajectory to the parlor is unorthodox. Upon the close of the bedroom door, we cut to a high perspective—possibly a windowsill on the first floor—from where we look down on rose beds, following as Michael sprints clumsily past. He trips, and now we are down on the lawn to witness him juggling his shower gel and his unbuttoned trousers and jacket. We cut to an interior shot: piano music is heard, and a waiter is walking toward the camera through a doorway on the other side of a room containing a chandelier, large oil paintings, and a parquet floor. The camera pans somewhat unsteadily to catch Michael as he runs in slapstick fashion from left to right across the space. Then Michael crosses the threshold between this public room and the next, and a camera is there in the next space to capture him, this time from above, as he comedically vaults over a male guest sitting slumped before the piano. Michael's trajectory through the house is thus witnessed alternately from above and from ground level.

However, the third room Michael passes through is introduced with a close-up of an oil portrait that the camera seems to be studying intently. A crash announces Michael's entrance stage left, and the camera performs a whip pan to catch him as he careers through the space. He has donned his dinner jacket but is still, inexplicably, grasping a tube of shower gel. We follow Michael at close quarters as he breathlessly approaches the door to his rendezvous (and has the presence of mind to hide the shower gel in a planter). Just as he straightens his tie and reaches to open the door, the male guests spill out. A peremptory conversation with his father in which he is invited to join the Masonic Lodge is dominated by another oil painting looming over Michael's right shoulder. This sequence concludes as the start of the party proper is signaled theatrically: white paneled doors open before the camera, which passes through this door along with the waitstaff with their trays of aperitifs.

This sequence establishes once and for all that these cameras *lurk*. They tend to lurk in thresholds, but sometimes they lurk studying objects, such as paintings. Some scenes are witnessed through glass window panes, the consequent blurred effect and muffling of sound substituting for similar postproduction effects. For example, before the start of the party, through a window we see Helge chasing a little boy across the lawn. With a creak, we cut to a close-up of a door opening, into a corridor where the clearly thrilled boy's task is to bash a pair of cymbals together and wake up the guests for dinner. Earlier, a blurred, slow-motion shot from inside the en suite bathroom shows Helene and Lars stripping dust sheets off furniture; Helene returns the gaze into the bathroom through the doorway, appearing to see something; the floral curtain in the bathroom window flaps suggestively in the breeze.

This establishes a visual trope of billowing drapes, gesturing to an unseen presence. The camera seems to get caught up in the floral curtain fabric while moving to join Helene on the floor during her search for the clues her sister has left. Later, the sight is again echoed in successive long-shots of Christian and his father's confrontation in the dining room. Floor-length curtains move gently in the evening breeze.

This emphasis on the house's architectural thresholds is mirrored—quite literally—in the various instances in key scenes of the reflection and refraction of light. Again, the pattern is established early on as associated with the "presence" of the dead sister. During her exorcism of the bedroom, Helene grips the molding of the bathroom doorframe as she steps apprehensively across the threshold of the apparently haunted space where her sister drowned herself. As she does so, her taut face can be glimpsed in the mirror beyond. The public rooms of the hotel are full of mirrors, too. At six o'clock, the guests gather in a drawing room to hear the opening speeches. First the toastmaster, Helmut, then Helge, stand in front of a large mirror, so that the listening guests can be seen reflected over each man's shoulder. Thus we see the individual reactions to the speech reflected both behind Helge and face-on, as the camera slowly zooms in to focus on Christian's face, behind his mother and brother. This conceit is used again as Christian begins his speech. A relaxed Michael is listening to him, drink in hand; behind Michael is a wood-framed mirror in which Christian can be seen in profile, beside a large glowing lampshade. Another example of the film's prevailing interest in playing with reflective surfaces comes as Michael and Michelle confront each other in an en suite bathroom. The camera films from inside the shower enclosure, angled so that it reflects another, mid-length, reflection in a mirror at ninety degrees to them above the wash-hand basin. This produces a subtle effect of "double exposure."

The way out of this hall of mirrors and untraversable thresholds opens up with the departure of Christian's parents after Helene's final, revelatory speech. The benighted toastmaster suggests dancing and coffee next door. Christian gets up to leave and, with the head and shoulders of a shocked female guest in the foreground to the right of the screen (as discussed in chapter 4), we watch Christian stagger through the open doorway, then through the adjacent space, and into the next room through the next doorway. Two sets of doors are now standing open. The threshold has been crossed, but by Christian, not the camera; the camera sits calm and still to witness the empty space that Christian has moved through.

Cinema's Architectonics

Giuliana Bruno insists that what architecture and film have in common is "the inscription of an observer in the field." We understand filmic space as we understand physical space, and our apprehension of each informs the other: the embodied observer is "a physical entity, a moving spectator, a body making journeys in space."[14]

In chapter 4, we saw how the mobile camera is implicated in the "taking place" of events: the camera does not simply record a preexisting reality but cocreates it from the inside. In the present chapter, we have seen how insofar as the camera is in on the action, it shares with the protagonists their status as guests: the space of the hotel remains unfamiliar, disjointed, fragmented. The guests "take place," but they do not inhabit the space. They are allotted hotel rooms for the night, but these spaces, even if they are not public, are certainly not private: they can be invaded at will by staff confiscating car keys to prevent escape from the unfolding nightmare or by ex-lovers seeking a place to fight. Our understanding of this space as architectural *and* filmic is limited.

This is a function not just of the camera but also of the editing and, ultimately, the cultural connotations of the medium. The quickfire editing in *Festen* not only denies the viewer any sense of the continuity of hotel space but also succeeds in rendering the ephemerality of hotel visitations. The extreme physical maneuverability of Dod Mantle's "weapon" cameras explodes space by shooting from angles and moving at velocities that would otherwise be unfeasible. The curious liminality of the space-time of a hotel that doubles as family home emerges in this place whose hidden spaces can be minutely explored (sports bags, painkiller tubes) but whose architectural and lived coherence remains ungraspable.

There is a more romantic reading of the fractured hotel space, which is to say that its disconnections give expression to the spectral point of view of the dead sister, Linda. We return to the idea of *Festen*'s ghosts in the third section of this book. Suffice it to say for the moment that there are incidents in the film where causality seems to act independently of spatial possibility. These include Helene's shout of "boo!" at one end of the house seeming to jolt Pia out of her bath and cause Michael to fall over, and Christian and Pia's apparently telepathic connection as she looks out of a bedroom window and he gazes into the darkness of the forest. At such moments, not just causality but also intimate communication seems to act independently of propinquity. The space-time continuum in this strange hotel is not shattered but complexly enfolded.

The discussion above covered how the camera is attracted to mirrored and reflective surfaces and, on occasion, lingers on paintings. One might muse that the film text is foregrounding the digital condition, which, as we know, Manovich sees as analogous to painting and which Vinterberg later played with in *It's All about Love*.[15] But there is another variety of "screen" surface that is featured, in its own unassuming way, more than almost any other in *Festen*. This "screen" is the silk tapestry that hangs behind Christian at the dinner table. Two of the walls in the dining room are hung with eighteenth-century silk tapestries sewn by an ancestor of the current owner. These depict harbor scenes, in Copenhagen and Glückstadt. In fact, the (real) dining room is called the Gobelinstuen, or Tapestry Room.[16] While the full scale of the tapestries can only be seen briefly in the film on one or two occasions as serving staff enter the room, a detail of the tapestry behind Christian is in shot during much of his speeches and shows the mast and rigging of a ship. Similarly, during Helene's speech, the tapestry on the wall behind her can be seen in some detail. The scale and shape of the tapestries—covering the walls like giant screens onto which the finely detailed harbor scenes are projected—reminds us how cinematic ways of seeing are rooted in earlier arts.[17] This is a matter of the shape and scale of the screen, but also of the finely worked surface texture of the silks. Inherent in film, as in its predecessors in the plastic arts, is the possibility of seeing haptically, that is, using the eyes as organs of touch. It is to the texture of *Festen* as moving image that we turn in the next chapter.

Conclusion

The first rule of the Dogma 95 Vow of Chastity insists that the film be shot on location and that props and sets must not be brought in. This rule necessitates that complex and well-equipped spaces must be found for each film, and the organization of the space in question will inevitably leave its mark on the narrative. However, there is a more complex relationship between film text and location, which can best be grasped by taking into account the similarities between, on the one hand, the construction of a space on-screen through (primarily) camerawork and editing and, on the other, the individual's apprehension of a space through which he or she physically moves. The affinities and lines of influence between the organization of spaces in art and the organization of art in space have exercised a range of critical theorists wishing to account for a viewer's experience of the encounter with on-screen (or virtual) space. In the case of *Festen*, camerawork and editing establish the hotel as discontinuous, both private and public, possibly inhabited by ghosts, and merely passed through by guests. The camera's intimate relation to the bodies in the hotel, as discussed in the previous chapter, is now seen to be complemented (or complicated) by another mood: it lurks in corners and on thresholds and constructs a fragmented space, the invisible dimensions of which it gestures to via the reflections and refractions of mirrored and glass surfaces.

6

Sense Memory and the Haptic

The inhabitation of space is achieved by tactile appropriation.
—Giuliana Bruno, *Atlas of Emotion*

Touching Objects

Festen feels its way from a fractured space divided by skewed and canted architectural lines and untraversable thresholds, toward a connected space more akin to the neoclassical principles that underpin the manor house. As Linda's ghost is exorcised and takes its leave, we, with the remaining siblings, begin to apprehend and appropriate the measured, rational, symmetrical space. But living bodies do not move through houses without leaving a trace: they scatter corporeal debris and make their marks. If we reflect (pun intended) on those polished mirrors and pristine glass surfaces in which so much of the party and its altercations are refracted, we might be tempted to sully them with our fingerprints. This chapter traces what Bruno calls the "tactile appropriation" of space, paying attention to all the senses—especially touch, but also hearing, taste, and smell—in their interaction with the visual.

There is a delicious moment as Helene, Pia, and Gbatokai collect glasses from the debris-strewn dining room for their little after-party in the next room. Helene comments that they should just take used glasses, "as long as it isn't a disgusting guy's glass."[1] This remark instantly conjures up the tangible effects of a night's drinking: the greasy traces of the drinker's lips and fingers on the glassware. These glasses are anodyne hotel property that has been "marked" by the saliva—the very DNA—of one or more guests.

According to the Dogma 95 rules, all props must be available in the place where the film is being shot. This rule seems to have been followed scrupulously in the production of *Festen*, if Vinterberg's "confession" is taken at face value. Even the appropriation of materials at the location is considered a sin. For example, as Vinterberg states:

> I confess to having set in train the construction of a non-existent hotel reception desk for use in *Festen*. It should be noted that the structure consisted solely of components already present at the location.
>
> I confess that Christian's mobile or cellular telephone was not his own. But it was present at the location.[2]

The confession also reveals Vinterberg's complicity in the purchase of clothing by some actors for use during the shoot. Taken to its logical conclusion, this principle means that all objects and artifacts crucial or incidental to the plot originate either as possessions of the actors or as property of the hotel. If the latter, they hover uneasily between affectless commodities of the hospitality industry and meaningful objects invested with memory or identity.

Laura U. Marks writes persuasively of the role of "objects of memory" in visual culture. She proposes the idea of the cinematic "transnational object," which she defines as any material thing that retains or accumulates "personal or ritual meaning" on its passage through different spaces.[3] Cinema can trace the journey itself, or it can excavate the material history and presence of the object. Material things can be invested with individual or collective memory, a potential source of multisensory information, and this potential can be fulfilled in interaction with the camera. Marks detects a "mournful quality" in images where visuality becomes tactile or haptic, for "as much as they might attempt to touch the skin of the object, all they [the images] can achieve is to become skinlike themselves."[4] Marks's notion of the haptic is rooted in her wish to account for how film and video by diasporic filmmakers and artists can communicate through recourse to all the senses, rather than through natural or cinematic language, thus subverting dominant Western cinematic practices and conventions. For Bruno, in contrast, the haptic in cinema is about motion, emotion, tactile inhabitation, and appropriation (thus exploring the image's depth), as well as surface texture. What may be said to link these diverse approaches to the same art-historical concept is summed up by Jennifer M. Barker in this way: "This kind of tactile perception of the world manifests itself in art that emphasizes texture and materiality—the grain of video imagery, for example—and encourages the viewer's gaze to move horizontally over the image, like fingertips caressing a particularly lush fabric or the dry grain of a sandy beach."[5] In our interaction with objects and textures on film, sense memories can be activated. Film cannot give us the direct experience of touch, taste, or smell, but it can gesture to these; Marks notes that film can approach such senses "asymptotically."[6] And so we respond affectively to such images.

There are numerous potential objects of memory and haptic surfaces in such a richly tactile environment as the Skjoldenæsholm hotel. There are certainly hands for us to feel with by proxy, too: Christian continually rubs at his fingers with a tissue; Pia's unwilling bottom is caressed by a randy female party guest; and Pia herself gently strokes the sleeping Christian's arm. Let's consider just three artifacts typically available in a hotel that make their way into the world of the film through a process of tactile appropriation: sheets, notepaper, and drinking glasses.

Cotton, Paper, Glass

One particular scene exploits the tension between the "found" set and its artifacts (props) and the affective potential with which meaningful props must be invested. Helene reluctantly agrees to take the bedroom in which her late sister, Linda, committed suicide, but she asks Lars, the receptionist, to come with her to the room to help fold up the sheets that still cover the furniture. From ceiling height, we witness Helene and Lars begin to pull dust sheets from the furniture. This is an apparently ordinary hotel bedroom, but the effect of the white sheets in the shuttered half-light is to diffuse the light over the various surfaces and to stir up patterns of dust and shadow as they are swept off the tables and wardrobes. Lars and Helene are performing a reclamation of the space, a kind of rational exorcism, a choreography of physical revelation that foreshadows the secrets that Christian will later unleash. The bedsheet, probably the most ubiquitous prop in any hotel, is here made to perform multiple functions. Visually, the sheets create abstract, quasi-haptic effects on the screen. Socioculturally, they speak of a particular socially determined practice of formalized mourning. Narratively, they suggest a literalized metaphor of revelation. Spatially, they transform the landscape of the room into a topography of folds and shadows, quite different from the glass and the smooth, dark mahogany that will be uncovered. Crisp white cotton, that tactile surface, recurs throughout the film, particularly in the form of the white shirts that the siblings don for their late-night party.

If the white sheets are blank surfaces onto which stories can be written or blood can be spilled, the fateful story is inscribed onto a different surface.[7] Linda's handwritten letter to her siblings—we might assume it was transcribed on-site, perhaps on hotel notepaper—passes quite literally from hand to hand, such that the asymptotic tension between untouchable object and viewer is intensified. We now follow the journey of this letter.

This object of memory—Linda's letter—is literally inscribed onto the fabric of the bedroom in red ink or crayon (or lipstick?). The game of *tampen brænder* (equivalent to the English "you're getting warmer") left by Linda for her siblings to play after her death plots a detailed exploration—by Helene and Lars and by the camera—of the angles of the room, before alighting on the hollow in the lampshade where Linda has inserted the letter. The last movements of Linda around the bedroom in which she died are thus retraced by protagonists, camera, and viewers, imbuing the object *at hand*—the hidden letter—with the physical and affective connection to Linda, and hence to her siblings, that is required to drive home its status as the preeminent object of memory in the film. The tension between the anodyne piece of paper and the weight of the handwritten words on it sutures the film narrative's present location to the suffering and death of the sister in this bedroom space, which we now understand to be very much inhabited.

Having found and read the letter, a panicking Helene stuffs it into her tube of headache pills, but the camera is there (lurking) at the end of the tube to witness this action. Pia later discovers it while looking for Helene's painkillers. It is passed back to Helene, via Christian, in a sequence that extends our exploration of the space of the manor house: the festive family conga line "borrowed" from Ingmar Bergman and, before him, Luchino Visconti.[8] A metal plate falling off the dinner table announces the beginning of the conga through the house. A camera waits below a table in a public room to witness the line emerging from a double door on the right. Helmut leads, flourishing a white napkin. We cut to a distinctive camera angle from inside a fire grate as the procession skips past, blowing imaginary trumpets, under the glowing chandelier. The line progresses upstairs and through a doorway; an aerial shot shows the procession moving through a smaller parlor with yellow upholstery, and then another angle on the celebrants is reflected in a mirror. A camera joins the procession as it moves through a doorway into the main staircase, where Christian is standing with Pia. He reaches out, apparently to the camera, with the crumpled letter. But a reverse shot reveals that it is Helene, now coming through the doorway, for whom he is waiting. A startling shot shows the letter from Christian's point of view, his finger holding it, directly in front of the camera. Helene reaches out to grab it as she passes.

In this sequence can be seen an instance where the camera's two behaviors are combined, as noted in chapters 4 and 5: the incorporation of the camera-operator into the action and the detached registration of movement through disconnected space. It seems significant that these two kinds of embodied spatial experience should meet and merge here at the pivotal point of the film: the literal "handing" of the letter from brother to sister.

Helene's relation to the letter remains intensely tactile, gesturing to the idea of skin on skin: when called upon to read it aloud, she pulls it out of her brassiere and is last seen clutching it loosely on the

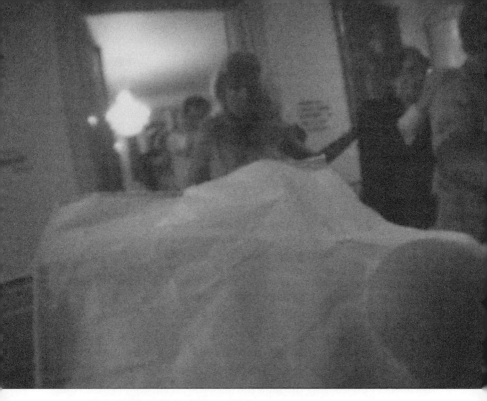

6.1   Christian hands the letter to Helene

table, stunned, as the consequences of its revelations play out. As we shall see later, the texture of the image during this speech incorporates the room into one thick parchment—or skin.

Arguably the most ubiquitous object in *Festen* is the drinking glass. Glasses are everywhere—this is a party in a hotel, after all—but their complex meaning belies their ubiquity. As we have seen from Helene's chance remark, glasses are marked with traces of the bodies that have been using them. The use of glasses in *Festen* is an unusually rich example of how an object can provoke an affective response in the viewer by activating a range of sense memories.

Liquid in glasses is established early on as a potent proxy for Linda's death by drowning. While Michael sings in his postcoital shower and Pia holds her breath under water in the bath, a barely discernible close-up of water swirling in Christian's glass imbues the tension of the moment with a sensuous, fragile feel until Helene's cry of "boo!" sends shockwaves throughout the hotel. Thereafter, used glasses are frequently employed as a smeared, fragile barrier between the camera and Christian.

On the level of taste and smell, glasses hold, of course, wine, and this is imbibed throughout the night. There is a particularly concentrated montage of wine-fueled debauchery from the point where the main course, venison and cranberry, is served: the guests clink glasses, discuss luxurious foods, and become increasingly inebriated, even to the extent of falling off their chairs. At points of crisis, a more extreme trigger is repeated: a protagonist takes great gulps of wine, far beyond the socially acceptable norm and beyond the bounds of physical comfort. Helene, for example, takes two slugs of wine as Christian begins to hold forth about "when Father took his bath." Christian himself ostentatiously drains two large glasses of red wine in quick succession as his mother publicly scolds him for telling lies about his father. The heady, burning sensation of the strong red wine in the throat is almost tangible, but must be "filled in" from memory by the viewer.

It must be acknowledged that *Festen* does not seem particularly interested in the food served during the dinner. It is by no means a "foodie" film, compared to, for example, its Danish predecessor *Babettes gæstebud* (Babette's Feast; dir. Gabriel Axel, 1987) or a film like Abdellatif Kechiche's *La graine et le mulet* (Couscous; France, 2007), whose handheld aesthetic owes much to Dogma and suggests how *Festen* might have constructed a sense of the taste, smell, and texture of the food in the same way as it gives us a strong sense of touch. Nevertheless, the shots of wine drinking in *Festen* are frequent, intense, and sustained enough to warrant consideration of how their impact on the viewer might function.

Where food and drink are concerned, taste and smell function in consort and notably so in our experience of a wine's bouquet. Taste involves a degree of breach of the body by environmental matter, but scents are peculiarly material, and smell is processed in the brain in distinct ways. Marks explains that olfaction is processed by the brain's centers for emotion and memory before it links to cognition; intensely emotional experiences therefore brand their associated odor into what Marks terms the "sensuous unconscious."[9]

It follows that responses to any given smell or taste—based as they are on personal sense memory—are likely to be peculiar to the individual, as well as culturally encoded: "The cultural meaning of smells is made in interaction with their location and with the previous experience of the one who smells."[10] This poses a paradox for the communication of the olfactory environment in audiovisual media: "As individual memory triggers, smells function better than audiovisual images. As communication, however, an audiovisual evocation of smell is, I believe, a more faithful representation than physical smells themselves."[11] The very materiality of smell, and to a lesser extent taste, makes it resistant to sublimation into collective cultural encoding, but film can exploit the potential intensity of individual sense memory to tease out a volatile affective bouquet.[12]

Metal on Glass

In terms of sound, the glasses constitute a crucial example of how the integrity of the pro-filmic world—the guarantee that the image is not produced apart from the sound, that the event happened as recorded—is largely supported by sound, not image. In this case, the social convention of tapping a glass with a knife or fork to announce a speech plays an important role in signposting the progress of Christian's descent into anger and grief. For the viewer (and for the guests), the sound of metal on glass becomes increasingly traumatic as the evening progresses. The conventional short series of clinking sounds that announces the first few speeches is echoed in two complex sequences in which Christian misuses the convention. Christian readies himself to speak again. He plays a scale on some glasses. Here, for his second speech, the editing matches the chimes: three jump cuts almost matching the rising notes as he moves from glass to glass. The sound functions in lieu of extra-diegetic sound, as the glasses are not in shot. Later, after a long standoff with his mother, whose chin starts to tremble as she repeatedly exhorts Christian to stand up and apologize to his father, Christian eventually gets up. The camera looks down at the array of tableware in front of him as he picks out a sarcastic tune with his knife on the glasses and reveals that she had witnessed the abuse and chosen to ignore it. More generally, if the proper use of cutlery, crockery, and glassware is a form of social control, the periodic piercing of the tension with the sounds of knocked-over glasses, dropped platters, and smashed plates articulates the social and emotional disintegration of the family.

We could go further than this identification of the aural impact of glassware and suggest that glass is the film's material metaphor for the event that is never seen: the sexual abuse. The film cannot approach, except asymptotically, the sensation of violent abuse, penetration, skin on skin, yet it can generate affective impact through gesturing to brittle, smeared, smashed glass—the crash, the breakage, the bloody penetration of the body that never comes in the film but is always threatened.

Intermediality and Decomposition

The artifacts in the pro-filmic space are not the only material things invested with sense memory and inviting touch. For Barker, Marks, and Bruno, the image itself, and its material instantiation, can be a haptic surface and invite a tactile appropriation. Here, we need to return to the matter of *Festen*'s medium and material, previously discussed in chapter 3.

It will be remembered that Vinterberg adopted digital video for the shoot only reluctantly. In the end, he admitted that digital turned out to be an appropriate medium for *Festen*, because its alleged "coldness" and "deadness" reflected the experience of the Klingenfeldt-Hansen family. Vinterberg took on the mantle of the first DV director reluctantly, ambivalently.[13]

Anthony Dod Mantle, director of Photography on *Festen*, has also spoken of his original wish to shoot on 35mm. Dod Mantle recalls experimenting with a range of film formats: 35mm, 16mm, even considering Super-8, before cost constraints hammered home the need to adopt video as the format. Crucially, Dod Mantle decided to "do something dynamic," rejecting conventional video cameras and adopting a first-generation home video camera, the Sony PC7E, whose maneuverability is discussed in more detail in chapter 4.[14] While the cameras provided mobility, the images they shot were also conditioned by the ban on artificial sources of light, as dictated by the Vow of Chastity. It was in the need to reconcile the images shot in often less than favorable lighting conditions with the transfer to 35mm that Dod Mantle found a new visual "language" emerging in the intermedial transfer between digital and analogue. Dod Mantle has spoken at some length about how this process pushed the image to the limits of legibility and imbued the image with a sense of inexorable disintegration or decomposition:

> You're talking serious decomposition here. You're talking words like "disintegration" and "destruction." But all those metaphors were appropriate for that disgraceful family. I just wanted to find a cinematic language that could convey that pretty catastrophic, pitiful—also amusing—situation these people were in. In the end, I converted the video to a very high-speed, pushed film stock. That way, the digital noise starts to speak to the film grain. And I wanted this square, Academy, organic mass to bubble up there on the screen, you know? I wanted to take a Vermeer and a Rembrandt, and get a big soup spoon and really stir 'em up, like porridge oats. That's what I wanted to marry off, progressively, through the film. It's hard to control, and I can't pretend I had complete control of it throughout.[15]

And again, elsewhere:

> I wanted an image tending toward decomposition as opposed to high resolution. This combined with the mobility and agility of the video camera was in dynamic terms close to pure organic film grain. Pushing exposure both in shooting and in transferring can enhance video noise to an interesting esthetic dimension.[16]

I quote these wonderful, boisterous accounts of Dod Mantle's aims and technique at some length because they encapsulate an important point about how the idea of the materiality of the film persists in this hybrid digital-analogue project.

Foregrounding the effects of intermedial transfer is, of course, hardly new. It had become a mainstay of avant-garde video art in the 1980s: artists would film on Super-8, 16mm, or other formats, transfer to video for editing, and scan back to 35mm for theatrical release. Most notably, this technique was used by Derek Jarman in, for example, *The Angelic Conversation* (1985) and by Peter Greenaway in *Prospero's Books* (1989).[17] Chris Meigh-Andrews sees the excesses of the mid- to late 1980s as "a period of over-enthusiastic self-indulgence" as video artists experimented with newly available processing technology. Many videos of the period, he says, "suffer from visual overkill and harshly processed vacuousness." In some cases, these were attempts to critique the effects of the contemporary information explosion.[18] An important precursor in the Danish context is Lars von Trier's *Medea*, made for Danish television in 1988. Von Trier's *Medea* was based on Carl Th. Dreyer's unrealized screenplay. Its self-conscious exploitation of the denaturing of the image inherent in video-to-35mm transfer—and back again for the purposes of television broadcast—enriches the viewer's instinctive grasp of the inaccessibility of the original legend through the layers of classical drama, Dreyer's screenplay, and the mists of cultural difference. The obviously manipulated, disintegrating images lead us to grasp the multiply mediated status of the tale and its antiheroine.

Similar interpretations of the "porridgy," pushed images can be applied to *Festen*. And yet the process at stake in this case is not perceptually or physically the same as with video-to-35mm transfer. The new factor in this first commercial attempt to transfer digital video onto film stock is the distinctive pixel matrix, which underlies the digital encoding of visual information. David Rodowick writes of this process that printing digital video to celluloid often magnifies the pixels. Even if this magnification effect is not obviously visible, it may be that the grid pattern of digital pixels is subliminally apparent.

This is because, as Rodowick explains, "a pixel array is like an image made of mosaic tiles: the position of the pixels is fixed, not random and shifting like projected film grain."[19]

As Dod Mantle suggests, and predictably enough, the image most obviously breaks up in this way toward the violent climax of the film, where light conditions are at their worst. As Michael continues to kick his father, the old man whispers either "you're killing me" or "kill me." At this point, the father is, literally, a "disappearing image" in Marks's parlance: a video that "flaunt[s] [a] tenuous connection" to reality, appealing to "a look of love and loss."[20] A less extreme, but more poignant, case of visual disintegration can be seen in the sequence in which Helene reads aloud her sister's letter. Here, the pixelation is apparent but is more diffuse ("porridgy," even) in the warm light of the evening lamps. At this moment of painful catharsis and reconciliation, the whole room has taken on the parchment hue of Helene's silk dress and the warm tones and textures of the wall tapestries. The tone and texture is suggestive of aged vellum, the material in which writing surface and animal skin meet.

The notion of haptic texture can also be extended, with a little goodwill, to sound. The rule that the sound must not be produced apart from the image leads to the inclusion of some shots where the sound is less than clear: rushing noises like tinnitus, overwhelming ambient sound in the dining room, unstable sound levels, apparent incoherence between sound level and location of source. All of these create a patina of non-naturalistic sound effects that are the literal equivalent of pixel "noise" and also stand in lieu of analogue indexicality as the guarantee of the integrity of the pro-filmic event.

Conclusion

Recent film theory has investigated how cinema, as an audiovisual medium, can activate the other senses in the viewer. Images do this by gesturing to the sensory information they cannot directly convey, but which can be "filled in" from sense memory. This is a particularly interesting process in *Festen*, because the first rule of the vow precludes any props being brought in, thus necessitating that standard-issue hotel equipment be invested with sensuous, multisensory meaning sufficient to bear the emotional weight of the film. In *Festen*, the hotel space and the artifacts it contains are subject to a process of tactile appropriation, which plays out in two main ways. First, various banal items found on location (bed linens, notepaper, wine glasses) are made to interact with bodies and cameras in ways that render them central to the construction of scenes of affective intensity, such as the suicide letter's discovery or the successive speeches. Second, the response of the camcorders to changes in light and sound levels is incorporated into the film, producing shifting audiovisual textures that interact with film grain in the final transfer to 35mm, thus investing the film image intermittently with a haptic quality.

Vinterberg's and Dod Mantle's trial and error with different syntheses of film and video took place on the cusp of a technological turning point and had a role in shaping cultural attitudes to how digital video *looked*. That Dod Mantle eventually settled on digital video for the shoot was a decision driven as much by economics as by aesthetics, but his response to this constraint was to invent a distinctive alchemy of digital and analogue. Thus, *Festen* can, in one sense, be interpreted as a harbinger of the "death of film" by dint of its adoption of digital image capture. Nevertheless, its adherence to the regulations of the Dogma 95 vow ensure that the tropes of decomposition and disintegration that haunted film culture around the millennium emerge visually in the film text, its intermedial texture itself generating meaning. The film's flagging of its own material instantiation through the very breakup of the image into its digital constituents engenders a sense of the physicality and the mortality of the bodies that move through it. Appropriately, we now turn to greet *Festen*'s ghosts.

PART THREE

Festen's Ghosts

7

The Story of Allan

We don't know the truth. We are not in the truth business. We are in the storytelling business. Sometimes we hit what is more truthful than the truth.
—Mogens Rukov, "Adventures of a Productive Idiot"

The acoustics are unbearable: perhaps fifty people in a parquet-floored room full of crockery, cutlery, glassware. From between the guests, we focus on the blonde, handsome, thirty-something man, Christian. He glances nervously around the room. A guest's head ducks in front of the camera, blurred, to take a spoonful of soup. The camera moves to catch Christian in profile and jerks down to witness his barely touched soup, his water glass. Guests flirt, make small talk. Glasses are lifted. Voices discuss the soup. Lobster? Salmon? Tomato? A knife clinks on a glass. Christian raises himself up to his full height. Another camera catches him in profile against the diffuse light from the white muslin curtains. He takes a breath. In the kitchen, the chef announces: "The eldest son's speech!"

"It's nearly seven o'clock, and I would like to raise the first toast. That's my duty as the eldest son. Isn't that right, Helmut?" he asks the toastmaster. Now we are positioned behind Christian, looking down the I-shaped table to where his father and mother sit, directly opposite. From a low angle we turn to watch his face as he asks his father to choose between a green envelope and a yellow envelope. Again, the long shot down the table. As the father thinks about his choice, we see a colored envelope over each of Christian's shoulders. The father chooses green. Back to Christian's face. He is smiling. The green one is the interesting choice, he says. A sort of home truth speech. It's called "When Father Took a Bath." Cut to mother and father. The mother laughs a little too enthusiastically. The father looks a little apprehensive.

"Any Resemblance to Persons Living or Dead Is Purely Coincidental"

From the silky texture of the dining room as Helene voices Linda's letter, we move to another fabrication, a kind of moiré pattern of truths and untruths, where the tissue of lies makes the warp and weft of truth gleam more complexly. This story is Allan's story: told by a voice heard on the radio that inspired Vinterberg to start work on *Festen*.[1]

In March 1996, a thirty-four-year-old man settled himself in a blue chair in a recording studio in Copenhagen. He steeled himself for the interviewer's opening gambit:

> Allan, on your father's sixtieth birthday, you stood up and gave a speech. What did you say?

And out tumbled his response:

I told him a bit about my childhood, what he had done to me during my childhood, and what he had taken from me. Because now that everybody else had held speeches for him, I wanted to tell them that he hadn't been an angel all the time.

Koplevs krydsfelt, or *Koplev's Crossword*, was broadcast weekly between 1993 and 2006 on P1, the primary national radio station in Denmark.[2] Hosted by Kjeld Koplev, a journalist and author of children's books, the program teased out the life story of a different guest each week. On March 28, 1996, it was the turn of an ordinary thirty-something man, who chose to be interviewed under the pseudonym "Allan." A trained nurse and health-care manager, gay, and HIV positive, Allan had been invited to tell his story as a male survivor of incest. After the suicide of his twin sister, Pernille, who had also suffered many years of sexual abuse at the hands of their stepfather, Allan had resolved to make the truth about the family's troubled history public. And Koplev coaxed out his story, over the ninety minutes of the program.

A friend of Thomas Vinterberg was deeply moved by the radio interview and recounted it to the young director. Vinterberg recalls thinking that Allan's story was an extremely important one, because it not only tackled the taboo of incest but also dealt with the issue of family secrets and the mechanisms by which they come to light.[3] Later that year, he heard the radio program for himself, and in early December 1996, still angry and moved by the tale of abuse of Allan and his twin, he took the story to Mogens Rukov, who would later agree to coauthor the screenplay. Rukov snapped that he was tired of stories about incest and pedophilia, but he liked the idea of a film centering on the family parties he remembered from his childhood. The two men started work on what would become *Festen*, and the manuscript was finished by the following June.[4]

For cinephiles, the rest is film history—but for lawyers at Nimbus film, there was a very real possibility that the film might be "his"-story: that is, Allan or his stepfather might decide to sue for defamation. The standard disclaimer declaring the film's fictive status was included in the end credits, and Vinterberg followed legal advice to downplay the influence of the *Koplevs krydsfelt* interview in the press.

In the wake of *Festen*-mania, two different Danish journalists began to investigate Allan and his story. For the freelance writer Claus Christensen, it was a chance remark by an audience member at one of his public presentations in 1999 that sowed the seeds of doubt.[5] Why had none of the seventy-eight guests or staff at the "real" party come forward to comment on the resemblance between the film and what, for them, must have been at the very least a memorable evening? And why was Vinterberg so evasive on the origins of the story? Was it possible, the audience speculated after Christensen's talk, that Allan had been a "plant," a media stunt devised by Vinterberg or Lars von Trier to publicize *Festen*? Christensen decided to find out.

Christensen first listened to the tapes of Koplev's studio interview with "Allan," during which, over almost two hours, he recounts his memories of being abused by his hotelier stepfather and the impact on the family. The similarities between the details of Allan's story and that of Christian Klingenfeldt-Hansen are myriad: Allan and his twin sister are abused and raped over a period of many years by their stepfather. The abuse takes place over a sofa in the private office of the stepfather. The mother accidentally witnesses the abuse on more than one occasion but conspires in the silence. The twin sister gradually sinks into depression as an adult and ultimately commits suicide. There are step-siblings, too, whose lives chime with the characters of Helene and Michael. As Christensen wryly comments, it is with good reason that *Festen*'s end credits include the disclaimer "any resemblance to persons living or dead is entirely coincidental."[6]

It transpired that Kjeld Koplev himself had had some reservations about the veracity of Allan's story as it unfolded in the studio, but he had not asked his researchers to verify the guest's background.[7] All he knew for sure was that "Allan" was not a pseudonym but the interviewee's real name. After initially agreeing to work with Christensen to investigate the circumstances behind Allan's case, Koplev withdrew his support, for fear that his radio program would be discredited, along with other broadcasts on the subject of incest that were under development at the time.[8] By late spring 2000, Christensen had drawn a blank: the Copenhagen-based incest support group that had originally put Koplev in touch with Allan believed him to have died shortly after the interview was broadcast. Searches for death notices for Allan's twin sister, his mother, and Allan himself were fruitless. The hotel run by Allan's stepfather was unknown to contacts in the tourist industry. Christensen tracked down one trained health-care manager by the name of Allan in the appropriate age range; his voice was completely different from Koplev's Allan, and he denied all knowledge of the story. Christensen had not solved the mystery of Allan's identity, but his investigations had thrown up a new set of questions around journalistic responsibility. Is a program like *Koplevs krydsfelt* duty-bound to verify the truth behind its guests' stories? Or is its role more therapeutic, as Koplev explained to Christensen, with guests given the space and freedom to relate their life histories from their own subjective point of view? Christensen filed his story with the Danish weekly *Weekendavisen* for publication in May 2000, and after a minor skirmish about journalistic integrity with an irate Koplev in the pages of that same paper, he put the investigation on the back burner.

In the meantime, another Danish journalist, Lisbeth Jessen, had been making her own inquiries, with the aim of producing a radio documentary on the man whose story had inspired *Festen*. Fully six years after Allan's first appearance on *Koplevs krydsfelt*, Jessen succeeded in tracking Allan down in a small town in the south of Jutland. Over a period of several months, Jessen made a series of visits to Allan's home, taking Thomas Vinterberg with her on one occasion. The encounters between Allan, Jessen, and Vinterberg, together with extracts from *Festen*, were edited by Jessen into a finely wrought forty-five-minute radio montage for Danmarks Radio, titled *Efter "Festen"* (After *The Celebration*).[9] The genius of the documentary is that it exposes the listener to the same gradual erosion of belief in Allan's story that Jessen herself experienced; we hear for ourselves, as Allan talks, a man made articulate by anger and pain. We also begin, slowly, to identify gaps and illogicalities in the details of his story. For Jessen's investigation solves the mystery of Allan's identity, but it does so by allowing Allan the space to reiterate and embroider his story until, with the tape still rolling, the tale falls to pieces under the weight of his uncle's refusal to corroborate the "facts." Allan at last confesses that his history of incest and bereavement had been an elaborate fiction, woven at a time of personal distress. There had been no abuse and no dead sister. Invited to the studio, and prompted by Koplev to describe his confrontation at the party, he simply made it all up on the spot.

As Jessen later remarks, Allan's story may have been a tissue of lies, but it was nevertheless a thoroughly good yarn, convincing in its detail and in its delivery.[10] Perhaps the most poignant passages in Jessen's documentary are the exchanges between Allan and Vinterberg, during which the director, audibly moved by the encounter, gently presses Allan for the most exacting details of the scenario at the "real" party. Did he clink his knife on the glass to announce the speech? Which way did he face? What did he say? Having filmed his own version of the event, he has been trying to imagine how it really was for so many years, Vinterberg confides. It's incredible that someone can make a film that is so close to reality, Allan exclaims; *Festen* is so much like his own experience that it gives him goose bumps. Later, Vinterberg asks if he might see a photograph of Allan's late twin sister—he so much wants to know how she looked!—and Allan promises to send one. We hear how much the director longs to be privy to the material reality underlying the fiction he has committed to film. Little does Vinterberg know—or perhaps he already suspects?—that Allan is reimagining his "memory" of the speech in light of its iteration in *Festen*. Jessen had shown the film to Allan on her previous visit, and his whispered reactions are heard in the montage, interspersed with the film's dialogue. As the voice of Ulrich Thomsen, playing Christian, announces, "A toast to the man who killed my sister!" Allan murmurs, "My words exactly!" Jessen's documentary, then, captures the very moment of cross-fertilization between two fantasies: the world-famous film and the event it portrays, an event that never was.

Assessing the documentary a few years later, after Allan's untimely death in a car accident in 2004, Jessen ponders Allan's tangled web as symptomatic of the contemporary hunger for "real stories" in the media.[11] What is it in our culture that compels people to contact the media and perform this kind of story? she wonders. Why are journalists so easily seduced by audience appetite for traumatic tales of suffering and survival? One answer is the turn-of-the-millennium hunger for the real, the culture of anxiety about the ability of new media to capture reality, of which Dogma 95 is symptomatic, as discussed in chapter 1. Jessen is also fascinated by what Allan's case has to teach us about the tension between fiction and history and the impossibility of mediating unadulterated truth. Peter Schepelern has remarked on the irony that the first film of a movement that seeks to force the truth out of characters and situations is based on a lie.[12]

But is it perhaps too simple to dismiss Allan's story as a lie? Might we, instead, see it more generously, as a translation or fable of the all-too-real pain of bereavement? Dogma 95, Koplev, and Jessen, in their distinctive ways, seek to "reveal the truth"—and, in their own ways, they each reveal that the most compelling truth is to be found in fiction.

"Somehow, the Film Belongs to the Director"

After "The Celebration" won Jessen the prestigious Prix Italia for documentary / current affairs for 2003. Ironically, the story that won Jessen her prize was not the one she set out to tell. Like *Festen* itself, the brilliance of the story stems from the Promethean power of someone else's narrative. The circle, as Allan muses repeatedly in the documentary, is complete. But Jessen's deserved success on the back of Allan's narrative and confession leads us to think about another factor that renders the case of Allan so compelling: cultural anxiety about ownership of experience, an anxiety that has only become more acute in the information age. Put more prosaically, this is a question of intellectual property. Who owns Allan's story? Are Allan's rights over his narrative diminished by the discovery that it was fiction rather than remembered fact?

Leaving aside the concerns of Vinterberg's lawyers around the time of *Festen*'s premiere, integral to Jessen's documentary are questions connected to the concept of intellectual property. A telling remark at the beginning of a repeat broadcast of the program in 2007 suggests that one original motive for her investigation was a lingering feeling that Vinterberg had been gifted "a fully formed screenplay" by the (uncredited) Allan.[13] During Jessen's documentary, Allan has the sangfroid to complain that he is insulted by the disclaimer in *Festen*'s end credits that "his" story is fiction. Kjeld Koplev, too, remarks to Jessen in her program that he would indeed have liked his interview with Allan to feature in the end credits, though he had nothing against Vinterberg using the story: "We all stand on the shoulders of others," he muses.[14] For his part, Vinterberg wryly discusses with Allan his nervousness after the film's première, when, for months, he anticipated the phone call from Allan or one of the "real" party guests or, worse, the court summons from an irate, slandered father.

A sense of indebtedness haunts Vinterberg's heart-to-heart with Allan in Jessen's radio montage. As director, he says, he has allowed himself to be celebrated on the back of Allan's tragic and brave history; by way of a reward, he would like Allan to realize just how many people his story has touched and influenced. In the same vein, after Allan's eventual confession, Jessen gives airtime to Allan's fulsome apologies. But the economics of intellectual property still obtain: Allan owes Vinterberg only a "little apology," he thinks, because he must have thought that the story had something and has benefited from it. Jessen concurs: without Allan, she concludes, we wouldn't have *Festen*.[15]

Such a conclusion effectively ascribes authorship—or intellectual property rights—to the individual who concocts the core scenario. But there is a danger that this position belittles the work of those—among others, the director—who shape this raw material into finely wrought fiction. A more nuanced verdict on Allan's role is provided by Claus Christensen. In the wake of Jessen's radio program, Christensen wrote a follow-up article for *Ekko*, a Danish film magazine. With a few years' hindsight, he is less fixated than he had been on Koplev's arguably cavalier approach to the truth behind his guests' stories. What emerges from Christensen's 2003 article is an important truth about the narrative and intermedial intersections between the Koplev interview and *Festen*. His observation leads us to think through another dimension of the question of film "authorship," at least as it relates to Dogma 95: how material is shaped into a narrative and by whom:

> The mystery of *Festen* is solved. It wasn't a media stunt, or a conspiracy, or a sneaky bit of self-promotion, just a long chain of coincidences that eventually resulted in one of Denmark's greatest films. And several people contributed to the film's fantastic narrative. Allan provided the substance; Kjeld Koplev, an expert interviewer with a feel for the dramatic twist, coached him into the role of consummate storyteller; and Rukov and Vinterberg both shifted the focus away from the incest and toward the family party and the repression of secrets, and crafted a nerve-jangling plot.[16]

Christensen's conclusion about the genesis of *Festen*'s plot as an unwitting act of collective alchemy brings Allan and Koplev out of the shadows and into the circle of screenwriters, director, actors, editor, and other agents in the production process. This chimes with the logic of Dogma 95: if the director is not to be credited, then why not a form of distributed authorship? Crucially, Christensen is interested more in the form of the story than in its content ("true" or otherwise). He leaves aside the myriad details shared by the two fictive accounts of Allan/Christian's experience and astutely identifies the most crucial point of symbiosis between them as a detail of narrative structure.

As Christensen muses, Koplev's genius as interviewer is to find the dramatic turning point in his guest's story, the crux of the narrative, the question that will open the floodgates. In Allan's case, the interview begins by spotlighting the speech he remembers making at his stepfather's birthday party, a few months after his twin sister's suicide. From Jessen's radio program, we learn two things about the "archaeology" (as Rukov would call it) of this moment of creativity.[17] In Jessen's documentary, Koplev recalls chatting with Allan for around half an hour in the studio, trying to find the "hook." Allan claims he conjured the story of his speech on the spur of the moment, under Koplev's questioning. We might say, then, that the birthday party speech was a happy accident born of the chemistry between interviewer and interviewee. In Allan's fantasy world, his speech is the end of the party; the guests are horrified and scatter.[18] For Vinterberg and Rukov, however, the speech is the narrative big bang. It is so in two respects: Allan's speech triggers the creation of the screenplay, and Christian's speech is the narrative core of the film from which everything else unfolds.[19]

Conclusion

Mogens Rukov is fond of using the metaphor of archaeology to describe the layers of personal or collective stories and histories that emerge (or indeed remain unexcavated) in film. In a recent interview, he sums up how this approach can serve what he calls the "natural story":

> When you start on the story of a film, you have to work out what the story consists of. You try to progress the story, but really you're trying to dig down and find the qualities or the will that the character in the drama has. You're really trying to reveal what was hidden in that person. In that way, it's actually a historical investigation. It's the same as in literature, where you also use the past to ground the present.[20]

To borrow Rukov's metaphor, it is hard to imagine a story that requires deeper excavation through the strata of different lives and histories than Christian's story, which once was Allan's, which turned out to have its roots not in memory but perhaps in some more deeply buried trauma. The story of Allan's story, then, has become a saga in its own right. It poses questions about objective truth versus subjective experience and about the ethical obligations of different sectors of the media. It also has much to teach us about narrative transformations of material across different media and about concepts of artistic ownership or authorship as they are renegotiated for the digital age.

If the tenth rule of the Vow of Chastity is that the director shall not be credited, it seems only appropriate that attribution of authorship of the first Dogma 95 film is beset with uncertainty. We now follow the story on its journey into the hands of more coauthors and another manifestation: the theater stage.

8

Festen from Screen to Stage

It is because that infinity which the theater demands cannot be spatial that its area can be none other than the human soul.
—André Bazin, "Theater and Cinema"

Theater and Cinema

In late summer 2007, *Variety* magazine declared that the West End was "ready for its closeup": the new season in London's theaters was to be dominated by screen-to-stage adaptations.[1] A long list of productions encompassed long-running stage versions of Hollywood products such as *Dirty Dancing*, *Hairspray*, and *Desperately Seeking Susan*, as well as versions of "smaller, independent or foreign-language films."[2] Tom Cairns, in discussing his stage production of Pedro Almodovar's *Todo sobre mi madre* (All about My Mother; 1999), emphasizes the relative novelty of adapting films for the stage: "It's totally expected that a play will be constantly reinterpreted by different creative teams. The re-imagining of films is a relatively new development—nobody has quite decided how it should work."[3]

Three years earlier, in March 2004, *Festen* had opened to rave reviews at the three hundred–seat capacity Almeida Theatre in North London.[4] Before the year was out, it would transfer to the much larger Lyric Theatre on Shaftesbury Avenue in the West End and would be given at least partial credit for rejuvenating the London theater scene. Box office receipts in the West End reportedly showed a healthy 6 percent rise that year, bringing London's theaterland its hitherto most profitable year.[5] Although the production was less of a "hit" on Broadway two years later, the staging of *Festen* in the United States was the first instance "in modern times" of a Danish play making it to Broadway, it was reported.[6] Indeed, by summer 2006, around fifty different productions had been put on worldwide in twenty countries.[7]

Festen is a fascinating case study in this brave new world of stage adaptation of world cinema, where "nobody has quite decided how it should work." Not only was the direction of translation across media something of a novelty at the time, but we also have multiple versions of the stage play to examine, including a radical rewrite for the London stage by David Eldridge. Before looking at these dramatizations in more detail, though, it is instructive to consider film theorist André Bazin's comments on the ontological differences between film and theater. Bazin wrote perceptively and at length on the relationship between cinema and theater, but his essays repeatedly swerve away from countenancing the possibility of screen-to-stage adaptation.[8] Nevertheless, certain of his observations on the distinction between cinema and theater are of use to us in trying to puzzle out the remarkable "translatability" of *Festen* from film to stage.

The most fundamental difference between the two arts, for Bazin, is in fact not the presence or absence of the actor. Drawing on his conviction that cinema is first and foremost an indexical medium, he argues:

> It is false to say that the screen is incapable of putting us "in the presence of" the actor. It does so in the same way as a mirror—one must agree that the mirror relays the presence of the person reflected in it—but it is a mirror with a delayed reflection, the tin foil of which retains the image. . . . What we lose by way of direct witness do we not recapture thanks to the artificial proximity provided by photographic enlargement?[9]

Bazin goes on to explain that what is crucial to theater audiences is not the physical presence of the actors per se. Rather, it is the "reciprocal awareness of the presence of audience and actor," the actor, the human onstage, being the "mainspring of the action," for there can be no drama in the theater without actors (102). Meanwhile, cinema's mainspring is nature, the world, and thus involves no such reciprocal contract: we merely watch, in a dark room, "a spectacle that is unaware of our existence and which is part of the universe" (102). Bazin then turns to focus his attention on the creation of dramatic place in the theater. Rather than record and belong to the world as film does, theater takes place on a demarcated stage marked out from reality by its footlights:

> Founded on the reciprocal awareness of those taking part and present to one another, [theater] must be in contrast to the rest of the world in the same way that play and reality are opposed, or concern and indifference, or liturgy and the common use of things. Costume, mask, or make-up, the style of the language, the footlights, all contribute to this distinction, but the clearest sign of all is the stage, the architecture of which has varied from

time to time without ever ceasing to mark out a privileged spot actually or virtually distinct from nature. (104)

For a film adaptation of a theater play to succeed, then, and not merely be "filmed theater," the distinction between cinema and theater space must be resolved. In Bazin's words: "The trump card that the director must hold is the reconversion into a window onto the world of a space oriented toward an interior dimension only, namely the closed and conventional area of the theatrical play" (111). But what of the adaptation in the opposite direction? What of the journey of *Festen* from screen to stage? I want to suggest that Bazin's analysis holds good when reversed. That is, the success of *Festen* onstage can be attributed in large part to its treatment of the key ontological difference between stage and screen on which Bazin focuses: its reorientation of the coherent space of the Dogma 95 location toward the closed space of the stage.

Festen Onstage

The playwright Bo hr. Hansen, who had collaborated with Vinterberg on his early films, adapted the screenplay of Festen for the stage. Hansen has described the process as follows: "I wrote the play based on the (film) manuscript, and I needed of course to change a few bits and pieces, but I also enjoyed using material which hadn't made it into the final film. Thomas and Mogens read my drafts, commented, and approved them. . . . For me, it was like translating. That is: the material was there. It just had to be translated into another language: from film to theater language."[10] The play was first performed in Germany in 2001 and put on in France and Denmark the next year. In 2002, Rukov described the spread of the play across Europe in the wake of the film's success at Cannes:

> Soon we get a call. Somebody in Germany wants us to make the film into a play. We ignore him. We think it a small business. I think we don't understand the attraction of the story and the narrative. How can it be so important? Look at us. We are not important. Yes, Thomas is. But yet, again, we are not. We are little people.
> The German continues. He gets his way. The play opens in Dortmund. The day after in Dresden. Now it's produced on the whole continent, in Scandinavia, in the Balkans. It just opened in France, in Bo Hr. Hansen's adaptation, very true to the original text, under our supervision.[11]

This dramatization is indeed very close, in terms of language and narrative shape, to the original film; many lines can be recognized more or less verbatim.[12] Scenes corresponding to the film's narrative begin in act 1, scene 3; they are preceded by two short scenes, the first of which shows Linda hiding her suicide note in a lampshade, and the second of which is a soliloquy from Helge on his hopes for the party. Linda is thus a little more prominent and "concrete" in the play than she is in the film: she appears in a dream sequence in act 2, scene 9, and again in the final scene, at the breakfast table, where she takes her leave of Christian.

Naturally, the architecture of the theater dictates that scenes which, in the film, take place outside the confines of the house must be relocated to the interior space of the manor. This entails, for example, Helene recounting her flirting with the taxi driver after her arrival (act 1, scene 4), and Linda appearing to Christian in the same space as the dancing or breakfasting guests, who are caught in a silent freeze-frame while Linda is present. The complex space of the hotel is thus concentrated into a single room dominated by a table. The list of characters specifies eight party guests, over and above the family and servants (though the individual production decides the number of guests onstage).[13]

In the United Kingdom, however, a new and distinct rewriting of the stage play was commissioned. This was the version that attracted such accolades in London and transferred to Broadway. Echoing the construction of Vinterberg as the "golden boy" of Danish cinema, no fewer than three "bright young things" in British drama were involved: David Eldridge adapted the play, Rufus Norris directed it, and Ian MacNeil was the scenic designer. This starry constellation, brought together by Canadian producer Marla Rubin after she saw Eldridge and Norris's previous collaboration on *Under the Blue Sky*, undoubtedly contributed to the "buzz" around the play during its extended London run in 2004. Norris reportedly approached Rubin with a request to direct, and much of the rest of the team comprised his long-standing collaborators, Orlando Gough (music), Paul Arditti (sound), and Katrina Lindsay (assistant director), as well as MacNeil as designer.[14]

Why was the revised version necessary for the British stage? Interviewed around the time of the Almeida opening, the thirty-year-old Eldridge explained that it was a matter of local theater culture: "In Europe, where there's a culture of director's theater, the directors tend to adapt the play while directing it. But here in Britain it's the writer who does the adaptation. Whereas European directors use a writer's work merely as raw material, in Britain the writer is king."[15] By all accounts, producer Marla Rubin had to persuade Vinterberg, Rukov, and Hansen of the need for an English rewrite, and during the yearlong writing process the Danish team—"generous and sharp-witted," says Eldridge—was closely involved in debating the shape that the new story eventually took. Eldridge was discouraged (though not forbidden) from reordering scenes, as the "natural" storytelling patented by Rukov—and the means of "forcing the truth out of characters and situations"—was considered paramount to the text as film and play.[16] The Danes also encouraged him not to rationalize the characters' actions too much.[17] Eldridge thanks Vinterberg, Rukov, Rubin, and Norris in the acknowledgments to his published stage play, dated February 2004, and copyright is attributed to Vinterberg, Rukov, and Hansen. Again, Rukov gives expression to the importance of the London project, as well as the willingness of the Danish writers to collaborate: "Next autumn, in London, there will be an English theatrical version. A London Opening, my God, what are the horizons? Where does it end? The producer Marla Rubin works hard on it. The dramatist David Eldridge works on an adaptation. We are in contact. We supervise. It will be an English drama and our drama."[18] Eldridge's *Festen* is markedly sparser than the Danish play. Dialogue is sparing; over and over again, the stage directions indicate "a slight pause" between lines. At times, this is designed to push the tension in the auditorium to its limits, echoing perhaps Harold Pinter's use of pauses.[19] For example, in act 2, scene 2, the directions read:

> *They begin to eat the meal—in complete silence.* Mette *watches* Pia, Michael *watches* Gbatokai, Helene *watches* Lars, Poul *watches* Helmut, Grandfather *watches* Else, Helge *watches* Christian. *After a little while the* Little Girl *appears. Helene calls her and she goes and sits on her lap. And the only sound apart from the meal is of her giggling and playing under the table.* Mette *lets her be. It is unbearable. Again this continues for longer than you think you can get away with. Suddenly,* Else *stands.* Helmut *clinks his glass and stands.*[20]

It will be noted that Eldridge's version includes a character referred to as the Little Girl. This figure effectively replaces Linda in the play; nowhere does the dead sister appear, but her function as bearer of memory of Helge's crimes and Christian's pain and loss is embodied in the Little Girl, who doubles up as Mette and Michael's daughter. The more workaday character Poul is an amalgam of various guests in the film and serves as comic relief. The Eldridge version has, then, a skeleton cast of fourteen, that is, those listed in the extract above, plus the chef, Kim. As Eldridge comments, this makes Helge's tyranny very easy to exercise at the intimate dinner—witness the crisscrossing of mutual surveillance in the above extract—and it also lets the complex and fascinating relationships between the siblings swim to the surface of the audience's consciousness.[21]

Over and above the narrative alterations, theater reviewers were quick to note the difficulty of adapting the Dogma 95 (anti-)aesthetic to the stage, and the codependency in this respect of the play and the staging: "Norris and his adapter David Eldridge have set themselves a tough task: finding a stage style that will achieve the power of the Dogme film. They give the piece a heightened realism. Scenes are played simultaneously, or they overlap, achieving a hallucinatory feel, which is intensified by Jean Kalman's sculptural lighting. We feel trapped in Christian's nightmare."[22] The lighting design for the production created a chiaroscuro or sculptural effect characterized by sideways-on lights often used in dance productions. The set was extremely simple, though it added a few items to Eldridge's stage directions: onstage were one wall, one door, a brick wall, twelve chairs, a dining table, and a bed.[23] As Sarah Hemming comments, this makes it possible for scenes to overlap. Indeed, Eldridge's stage play dictates that the stage serves simultaneously as three spaces in one at a key moment. This particular sequence is a salient example of how the London production recrafts the original Danish stage directions to reorient the fragmented filmic space of the hotel back toward Bazin's "closed and conventional area of the theatrical play."

In the film, the unwitnessed scene of Linda's suicide is suggested by an implied causal and spatiotemporal linkage between three events. The sequence in question connects three hotel rooms: Michael and Mette's epic fight and lovemaking, Christian and Pia's conversation and her bath, and Helene and Lars hunting for Linda's letter in her shrouded room. In a series of crosscuts between hotel rooms, the editing establishes the simultaneity of Michael's postcoital shower, Pia holding her breath under water in the bath (thus reenacting Linda's suicide), and Helene's first reading of the letter. So that Lars does not guess the letter's content, Helene distracts him by shouting "boo!" As she does this, fast cuts show Michael slipping and falling in the shower and Pia emerging, shaken, from the water. The implication is that Helene's shout has vibrated through the house, disturbing Michael and Pia. This is of course not impossible, but unlikely in such a large manor house. Palle Schantz Lauridsen, in his analysis of this sequence, suggests that "what is suggested by the editing when Michael falls in the shower, when Christian loses his glass, when Pia suddenly breaks out of the water in the bathtub is that the discovery of the letter is important to everybody—beyond causality."[24] We could go further, as I did in chapter 5, and argue that conventional space-time does not seem to apply in the hotel and that causality operates across apparent gaps and thresholds. The sister's death, in water, resonates through the watery spaces of the house.

In Eldridge and Norris's stage play (but not in the original Danish play or in other international translations) the space of these three hotel bedrooms and bathrooms is collapsed into one room, furnished by one double bed. On and around this bed, the three "couples" simultaneously climb to search for the letter, fight and make love, reminisce about the old days. Each pairing is, seemingly, unaware of the two other couples; their spoken lines and their movements are carefully choreographed to weave through one another. What we have here is a distillation of the film's subtle hints that space might work more through enfoldment than continuity; the stage is entirely what Bazin calls "a privileged spot actually or virtually distinct from nature." Another aspect of this sequence in the film is abstracted onstage, too: its use of water to make all three rooms cohere is, literally, echoed in the looped sounds of running water and children's laughter that characterize the sound design. "It never ends," is Christian's mantra in this play: the recursive trauma of abuse, the compulsion to replay the traumatic memory, is reiterated in the looped sounds, the Little Girl as Linda reborn, and the closed-off, atemporal space of the staged drama in its concentric bedrooms.

Encore: New York, Bucharest, Vienna

In April 2006, the London production premiered on Broadway in the presence of Vinterberg and the then Danish minister for culture, Brian Mikkelsen. The play, however, received a lukewarm reception in New York. This has been attributed to the cast trying too hard to be sympathetic, rather than stiff and cold.[25] Also advanced as an explanation for its short run of only forty-nine performances was an inherent cultural incommensurability between the style and subject matter and the American audience's sensibilities: every night, someone left the theater in shock, it was reported.[26] At the time of the Broadway opening night, Vinterberg was quoted as commenting happily: "It is as if I've sent a child out into the world. It's managing really well, and I don't have much to do with it anymore, but it's fantastic to see how well it's doing."[27]

With the passage of years and the proliferation of productions, the play seems to have established itself as a modern classic, independent of the film from which it was adapted. One recent example of a production staged in London amply demonstrates that the film is not necessarily acknowledged as an intertext by company or audience. A Romanian company, Nottara Theatre, brought its production of Bo hr. Hansen's text, directed by Vlad Massaci, to London's Barbican in November 2011.[28] This production was performed in the round, around a large dining table. It incorporated two video cameras and monitors into the set, so that three alternative perspectives on the action were available to the audience at any given moment. The cameras were usually focused in close-up on the faces of one or more actors reacting to the ongoing dialogue. They were mounted on tripods, so there was no camera shake, but the interest in close interaction with the faces of the actors recalled to some extent the aesthetics of the film. Indeed, the actors replicated certain recognizable gestures from the film's close-ups, such as Christian making faces with a spoon in his mouth. Curiously, though, when questioned at the postshow discussion, the director and actors denied that their intention was to incorporate a homage to the film into their play. Also telling was director Vlad Massaci's insistence that the play had been received in Romania as an obvious metaphor for the "rape" of the nation by Communism; the Romanian theater tradition of building two levels of meaning into its productions transformed the text into national allegory, he explained.

In any case, as we know from chapter 2, by 2010, Vinterberg was feeling the weight of *Festen* around his neck. He had, though, found a way to exorcise that particular ghost: together with Rukov, he had written a new play titled *Das Begräbnis* (The Funeral) for an Austrian theater. The play returns to the Klingenfeldt-Hansen family hotel ten years on, for Helge's funeral. Vinterberg explains why he set about writing such a sequel: "I felt that it wasn't true to say that with one speech, one night, you could ride off to Paris with the princess and half the kingdom. So when they come home ten years later for the father's funeral, I dive down into the bacteria that must still be in their bodies. And I let it develop into a real plague within the family."[29] *The Funeral* was Vinterberg's debut as a theater director, and he reports finding the experience extremely gratifying: easy, creative, and fun. He comments that theater can do things that film cannot, but in the same way as Dogma 95 could: as an "acute statement" with "living creatures in front of you, and a good story." Will *The Funeral* be adapted to film, thus squaring the circle? That remains to be seen, says the director.[30]

9
Media and Time

Mechanically reproduced images supposedly lack aura, but as images decay they become unique again: an unhappy film is unhappy after its own fashion.
—Laura U. Marks, "Loving a Disappearing Image"

With its echo of the first line of Tolstoy's *Anna Karenina*, Laura U. Marks's remark about the inevitable and idiosyncratic disintegration of every film reel or videotape is as if tailor-made for *Festen*, whose family is very definitely unhappy in its own way. But Marks was writing in the late 1990s, in that three-year period between Dogma 95's launch and *Festen*'s premiere. Published in the same year that the first DVDs were made commercially available, Marks's intervention came a little too early to appreciate how ephemeral the new medium would quickly turn out to be.[1]

While writing this book, I have watched, fascinated and a little horrified, as my trusty *Festen* DVD has grown old and battered. There is a discernible scratch. The sound cuts out momentarily at a couple of key points. Is the picture more pixelated than it used to be? I can't tell. On a couple of occasions this year, class screenings have been delayed by the DVD's refusal to display subtitles when played from any machine but my laptop. The DVD is malfunctioning. A more fastidious teacher would have invested in a new copy. And yet, and yet . . . I am unspeakably attached to this DVD, which, alone of all the workaday discs on my shelves, has emotional resonance. My sister found it in a branch of the now defunct and much-loved British chain store Woolworth's, the same weekend we went to see *Festen* at the Lyric Theatre in 2004. I willed it to last through the writing process. It did. I will buy a new one before my courses start next year.

Is it bad practice to write a book using a worn-out DVD? The suspicious reader may fret that my interest in Anthony Dod Mantle's "porridgy" images would never have been piqued had I been working with a brand-new disc. How can I be sure that every purported jump cut is not the DVD jumping? To this I would say, has any commentary on any film ever been written in the sure and certain knowledge that the medium in which the film text was instantiated was not defective in some way? Rodowick has written nostalgically of the pre-video days of his scholarly career, when projection in cinema theaters was still the only way to see films, and titles that were not on general release had to be tracked down. "Film history was a pursuit founded on scarcity," remembers Rodowick, and thus "the materiality of the cinematic experience was tangible."[2] For Marks, teaching with video in the early 1990s was a frustrating experience: "When I began to teach film studies I realized that the students will never 'really see' a film in class: it's always a film that's half-disappeared, or a projected video that just teases us, with its stripes of pastel color, that there might be an image in there somewhere, that there once was an indexical relationship to real things, real bodies."[3] However, she goes on to warn against regarding film on other formats as "a mnemonic for the ideal film, the Platonic film, once seen in 35mm in a good theater." For, as we have seen, slow erosion was also built into nitrate and its sister technologies. There is no urtext; we can no more access those "real bodies" or "real events" on screen than we can access "the truth" with which the Dogma 95 manifesto smirkingly teases us. With the advent of the digital, if the proliferation of "digitally remastered" versions of classics whets the desire for the ultimate "director's cut," the ubiquity of "extras" on DVD—outtakes, interviews, paratexts—evinces the contingency and arbitrariness of any text. As shooting on digital video became viable, the need to count the costs of film stock was obviated; unlimited hours of footage could now, in principle, be captured, for it was measured in bytes, not feet.[4]

Thus *Festen* has its ghosts, and they are so insubstantial that they did not fall to the cutting-room floor; they may yet exist, somewhere, nowhere, as digital code. It is known that Rukov and Vinterberg, early on in the writing process, agreed to "add the supernatural wherever we can."[5] But most of the alterations between manuscript and finished film, they later reflect, tone down the supernatural. Gbatokai was intended to be psychic, whereas in the final cut of the film, he is merely intuitive. The screenplay includes an extended sequence in which Christian becomes delirious in the woods, but Vinterberg and Rukov comment that in the film "the madness is in the cutting."[6] The fevered dream during which the smiling apparition of Linda hugs her brother was originally intended as an incestuous ménage à trois between Christian, Pia, and Linda. We have also seen how David Eldridge's rewriting of the Danish play resurrects bodily the figure of the abused child, who is conspicuous by her absence in the film.

It is Christian's hallucinatory dream of his ghostly sister that I would like to explore in this last chapter of the book, by way of a conclusion. The sequence is often cited as the point where *Festen* most flagrantly breaches the spirit of the Dogma 95 rules, if not the letter.

In pushing to its limits the seventh rule—"temporal and geographical alienation are forbidden"—the dream sequence also has much to tell us about how *Festen* exorcises its ghosts, or its trauma, and how films can be ghosts, too.

Christian's Dream

Helene has read her sister's letter to the assembled guests, putting to rest any lingering suspicions that Christian might be lying. A shell-shocked Helmut has suggested dancing and coffee in the adjoining room. Christian gets up to leave the dining room, and, in a shot we previously discussed in chapters 4 and 5, we watch him move through the adjacent space. Two sets of doors stand open, reminiscent of an interior by the Danish painter Vilhelm Hammershøi.[7] This is a cathartic moment: Christian is crossing a threshold into a space of light. While the guests begin to dance, the linear temporal connections between successive shots start to break down. Christian staggers to Lars at the reception desk and asks for a glass of water. Christian falls; Lars helps him to his feet. A low-angle shot shows Christian looking dazed, and the sound of wind in the camera's microphone is heard, suggestive of tinnitus or general disorientation. The noise disappears with the next cut, which is another disorientating shot as Christian sways. He falls to the ground. There follows a sequence of shots that transport us through the comatose Christian's dream to a later point in the narrative, subsequently timed at around three in the morning by Helene. First, there is darkness. The clicking of a lighter. A young woman appears, smiling, pretty, short-haired, in the glow of the flame that has been ignited. Lars runs for help. Christian lies on the ground, the camera beside him. Darkness. The woman whispers his name. He walks through the darkness in search of her. She whispers his name again. A loud, electronic trilling sound is heard intermittently. Christian flickers into view in the dark again. He wakes. He calls out for Pia. She is lying beside him. Again, the trilling sound. He gets up; he tells Pia that his sister is here and that he loves her (but is he addressing Pia—or his sister?). More trilling. His sister smiles kindly. He flicks the lighter again. We see a blurred light, a pool of whiteness in the dark. He walks through the darkness to a doorframe, where his sister stands, her hand on the molding. They whisper how much they miss each other. "Shall I come with you?" asks Christian. The electronic trill is insistent. A reverse shot. Linda shakes her head, smiles, no. She has to go now. They hug tightly. She caresses him. Darkness. Then the twins again. Then darkness. A white-paneled door appears in the black; it is slightly ajar, and behind it is a light. There is stillness. A shape staggers into the light, apparently from out of bed, pulling on his underpants. It is Christian; he lights a lamp and answers the ringing telephone.

This sequence manages not to defy the seventh rule through the very simple conceit of suturing Christian's dream to the "real world" via the trilling of what turns out to be the telephone. Every viewer will have experienced the segue between dream and waking life during which the sound that awoke him or her is incorporated into the dream. The temporality of the dream, while it continues, often bears little relation to "real" time. The dream sequence is thus time out of time—at once concentrated into the moment of awakening and stretching indeterminately between Christian's drunken collapse and blackout at the reception desk and his eventual return to consciousness, in bed with Pia.

9.1   The bathroom door in Christian's waking dream

Awakening to Life

This sequence is bookended with the ajar doors of the drawing room and bathroom. The doors are distinctive in the classical simplicity of their design. At one level, their appearance is a function of the architectural environment in which *Festen* was shot. At another level, they ensure that the sequence is "haunted" by another ghost of Danish cinema: the resurrection scene toward the end of Carl Th. Dreyer's *Ordet* (The Word; 1955). My intention in invoking this and other intertexts is not to argue for a conscious quotation or line of influence but to read one scene against another in the hope of enriching them both.

9.2   Mikkel closes the parlor door in *Ordet* (The Word; dir. Carl Th. Dreyer, 1955)

In Dreyer's film, a young woman, Inger, has died in childbirth, leaving behind two daughters, a distraught husband, and an apparently demented brother-in-law, Johannes. She is lying in her open coffin in a light-filled parlor. Her family files in to say their good-byes. Her husband, Mikkel, begins to sob at the prospect of her coffin lid being nailed on. Assured by his father that Inger's soul has departed, Mikkel weeps: "But her body, I loved her body, too!" Encapsulated in his cry of anguish is the longing for the physical presence of the lost loved one, the longing that is the source from which springs Barthes's romantic treatment of the photograph in *Camera Lucida* and the urge to embalm the dead that, for Bazin, underlies the plastic arts. And *The Word* miraculously fulfills that longing by allowing Johannes to bring the dead woman back to life. At his command, Inger's clasped hands begin, at first barely perceptibly, to stir. Her eyes flicker open.

She is returned in body to her husband, who lifts her from her coffin. Inger utters the film's last word: "life."

As in *Festen*, the sequence in which the beloved is returned to life is delimited by architectural thresholds—the doors and windows—and also by a clear indication of its exteriority to linear narrative time, or "realist" time. Inger's death is marked by her brother-in-law stilling the pendulum of the grandfather clock, and her resurrection—mirabile dictu—mandates him to set the timepiece in motion again. As Rebecca Harrison has observed, the ticking of that clock in *The Word* is the ticking of frames through the projector. While the clock is stilled, we are outside the diegesis proper and have digressed into the medium of film itself.[8] For Christian, his return to consciousness goes hand in hand with a temporal reorientation: his (surviving) sister immediately tells him the time over the telephone. In the measured electronic ringing of that telephone, the temporality of the world outside has both intruded upon Christian's dream and emphasized its atemporality. It is worth remembering, as well, that the first seconds of *Festen* are dominated by the too-loud ringtone of a cell phone, playfully calling attention to the film's status as a text marked by its own technological instantiation. Awakening to life is accompanied, here, by an electronic fanfare, not a mechanical chiming.

In the case of both films, there is a strong sense that the resurrection or fleshly visitation is a manifestation of the cinema's propensity to work miracles. Before our wondering eyes, Inger's fluttering fingers transform the still image of the dead woman into the moving image of a breathing, living being. We believe in this miracle because the indexical quality of analogue film vouches to us that *that has been*.[9] What of *Festen*'s digital ghost? We might say that the apparition of Linda in the flesh invests the digital video camera with our faith in its ability to give life. This, after all, is the same camera whose nimbleness has gestured to Linda's presence and point of view throughout the film, despite our lingering suspicions as to the "realness" of the images it has produced for us.

Canonizing Film

As the technology of the moving image developed through the twentieth century, it trained us to see the world from ever-evolving perspectives. The advent of digital distribution had a similarly revolutionary effect on how we see cinema itself, as Laura Mulvey explains:

> At the end of the twentieth century new technologies opened up new perceptual possibilities, new ways of looking, not at the world, but at the internal world of cinema. The century had accumulated a recorded film world, like a parallel universe, that can now be halted or slowed or fragmented. The new technologies work on the body of film like mechanisms of delay, delaying the forward motion of the medium itself, fragmenting the forward movement of narrative and taking the spectator into the past. Whatever its drive or desire, this look transforms perception of cinema just as the camera had transformed the human eye's perception of the world.[10]

To write a book about a film is beginning to feel like a curiously anachronistic practice. Surely, within a few years, it will be commonplace to write books for e-readers with digital video sequences embedded, replacing the paltry few stills and screen grabs that one can beg, steal, or borrow from film archives and production companies. *The Word*, and the rest of Dreyer's oeuvre, is already enjoying a digital renaissance on the Danish Film Institute's impressively rich online resource

Carl Th. Dreyer: The Man and His Work (www.carlthdreyer.dk), launched in spring 2010. *Festen*, meanwhile, enjoyed, for a time, a web presence that is worthy of note here, at the end of this book, but which itself has now disappeared into the digital ether.

The online version of the 2006 Danish Cultural Canon website, mentioned in chapter 1, gave the visitor access not only to information about the film and its citation in the canon but also to a sequence from the film.[11] The selected scene was Helene's speech, or, rather, her reading of Linda's letter. This is a scene to which we have returned several times in this book. What does it mean to wrench this six-minute sequence from its narrative belays and display it in isolation on the web?

Arguably, this sequence can stand on its own as an encapsulation of the essence of the film. It spans the anonymous exhortation to Helene to give her speech by proxy, that is, to read aloud her sister's suicide note, through to Christian's unsteady exit. As Helene reads, we see a series of head shots, portraits of Helene, her father, and the now very drunk Christian pulling faces to inject some levity into an otherwise unbearably tragic moment. As the letter comes to a close, the camera pulls back to its established position on the windowsill overlooking the room. But it is, of course, clear that there are several cameras in play in this scene, for it is also a good example of a complex space created by crosscutting but sutured to a defined stretch of time by the guarantee that the sound has been recorded along with the image. Each new angle on the space is happening "now." Crucially, too, this is the narrative climax of the film. Prompted by Christian to explain *why* he abused his children, the father declares: "It was all you were good for." Finally, as discussed in chapter 6, this scene is also a sustained example of visual texture, the image decomposing into the same parchment hues as the letter itself, under the process of transfer from inadequately (but beautifully) lit digital video to 35mm. As Mulvey writes, it is the "relentless movement" and rhythm of cinema that robs it of the potential of the still images, of the photograph, to reveal its indexicality and therefore its direct, almost tactile, relationship to the dead one.[12] And though this musealized sequence on a loop, or images from the streaming server, did not constitute still images, it nevertheless, again in Mulvey's words, "restore[ed] to the moving image the heavy presence of passing time and of . . . mortality"—and here I would add: of their reversal. The aura, she says, is returned to these "mechanically reproducible media through the compulsion to repeat."[13] Thus *Festen*'s unseen trauma—Linda writing her suicide note, and her lonely death—found something of an afterlife on the web, canonized and replayed as a fragment of national cinema.

Appendix A: Dogma 95 Manifesto and Vow of Chastity

DOGMA 95

DOGMA 95 is a collective of film directors founded in Copenhagen in Spring 1995.

DOGMA 95 has the expressed goal of countering "certain tendencies" in the cinema today.

DOGMA 95 is a rescue action!

In 1960 enough was enough! The movie was dead and called for resurrection. The goal was correct but the means were not! The new wave proved to be a ripple that washed ashore and turned to muck.

Slogans of individualism and freedom created works for a while, but no changes. The wave was up for grabs, like the directors themselves. The wave was never stronger than the men behind it. The anti-bourgeois cinema itself became bourgeois, because the foundations upon which its theories were based was the bourgeois perception of art. The auteur concept was bourgeois romanticism from the very start and thereby . . . false!

To DOGMA 95 cinema is not individual!

Today a technological storm is raging, the result of which will be the ultimate democratization of the cinema. For the first time, anyone can make movies. But the more accessible the medium becomes, the more important the avant-garde. It is no accident that the phrase "avant-garde" has military connotations. Discipline is the answer... we must put our films into uniform, because the individual film will be decadent by definition!

DOGMA 95 counters the individual film by the principle of presenting an indisputable set of rules known as THE VOW OF CHASTITY.

In 1960 enough was enough! The movie had been cosmeticized to death, they said; yet since then the use of cosmetics has exploded.

The "supreme" task of the decadent film-makers is to fool the audience. Is that what we are so proud of? Is that what the "100 years" have brought us? Illusions via which emotions can be communicated?... By the individual artist's free choice of trickery?

Predictability (dramaturgy) has become the golden calf around which we dance. Having the characters' inner lives justify the plot is too complicated, and not "high art." As never before, the superficial action and the superficial movie are receiving all the praise.

The result is barren. An illusion of pathos and an illusion of love.

To DOGMA 95 the movie is not illusion!

Today a technological storm is raging of which the result is the elevation of cosmetics to God. By using new technology anyone at any time can wash the last grains of truth away in the deadly embrace of sensation. The illusions are everything the movie can hide behind.

DOGMA 95 counters the film of illusion by the presentation of an indisputable set of rules known as

THE VOW OF CHASTITY.

I swear to submit to the following set of rules drawn up and confirmed by DOGMA 95:

1. Shooting must be done on location. Props and sets must not be brought in. (If a particular prop is necessary for the story, a location must be chosen where this prop is to be found).
2. The sound must never be produced apart from the images or vice versa. (Music must not be used unless it occurs where the scene is being shot.)
3. The camera must be hand-held. Any movement or immobility attainable in the hand is permitted. (The film must not take place where the camera is standing; shooting must take place where the film takes place.)
4. The film must be in color. Special lighting is not acceptable. (If there is too little light for exposure the scene must be cut or a single lamp be attached to the camera.)
5. Optical work and filters are forbidden.
6. The film must not contain superficial action. (Murders, weapons, etc. must not occur.)
7. Temporal and geographical alienation are forbidden. (That is to say that the film takes place here and now.)
8. Genre movies are not acceptable.
9. The film format must be Academy 35 mm.
10. The director must not be credited.

Furthermore I swear as a director to refrain from personal taste! I am no longer an artist. I swear to refrain from creating a "work," as I regard the instant as more important than the whole. My supreme goal is to force the truth out of my characters and settings. I swear to do so by all the means available and at the cost of any good taste and any aesthetic considerations.

Thus I make my VOW OF CHASTITY.

Copenhagen, Monday 13 March 1995
On behalf of DOGMA 95
Lars von Trier   Thomas Vinterberg

Appendix B. *Festen*: Data

Original title:	*Festen*
Alternative title:	*Dogme #1*
Country of production:	Denmark
Language:	Danish, English
Shooting location:	Skjoldenæsholm, Sjælland Denmark
Production company:	Nimbus Film, Produced in association with Danmarks Radio/TV by Svend Abrahamsen and Sveriges Television Drama (Sweden) by Johan Mardell, with support from Dag Alveberg at Nordic Film and Television Fund.
Length:	106 minutes
Format:	Printed: 35mm, Negative: Video (PAL)
Camera:	Sony PC7E
Aspect ratio:	1.33:1

Rating in Denmark:	Suitable for children aged eleven years and above.
Premiere:	June 19, 1998, at five Greater Copenhagen cinemas (Dagmar, Palads, Lyngby Teater, Grand, BioCity Tåstrup), plus ten provincial cinemas.
Distribution:	Scanbox
Director	Thomas Vinterberg (uncredited)
Director's assistant:	Eigil Jacobsen
Casting:	Rie Hedegaard
Screenplay:	Thomas Vinterberg Mogens Rukov
Producer:	Birgitte Hald
Line producer:	Morten Kaufman
Director of photography:	Anthony Dod Mantle
Additional photography:	Peter Hjorth
Editing:	Valdís Óskarsdóttir
Editor's assistant:	Vagn Rose
Sound:	Morten Holm
Boom operator:	Ad Stoop
Music:	Lars Bo Jensen
Stills:	Lars Høgsted

Cast

Ulrich Thomsen	Christian
Henning Moritzen	The Father
Thomas Bo Larsen	Michael
Paprika Steen	Helene
Birthe Neumann	The Mother

Trine Dyrholm	Pia
Helle Dolleris	Mette
Therese Glahn	Michelle
Klaus Bondam	Toastmaster
Bjarne Henriksen	The Chef
Gbatokai Dakinah	Gbatokai
Lasse Lunderskov	The Uncle
Lars Brygmann	The Receptionist
Lene Laub Oksen	The Sister
Linda Laursen	Birthe
John Boas	The Grandfather
Erna Boas	The Grandmother

Appendix C. Thomas Vinterberg: An Annotated Filmography

Sneblind (Snowblind; 1990, 48 min.)

Director, Executive Producer. Drug abuse blurs the boundaries between reality and images for a young cinema usher.

Slaget på tasken ([no English title]; 1993, 32 min.)

Director, screenplay. In this short film made for television, we see the actors who will begin to recur in Vinterberg's films; here, the cast includes *Festen* actors Ulrich Thomsen, Bjarne Henriksen, and Helle Dolleris. A young couple is awoken one morning by housing association functionaries, who take photographs to prove that the two are living there illegally.

Sidste omgang (Last Round; 1993, 43 min.)

Director, screenplay (with Bo hr. Hansen). *Festen*'s Thomas Bo Larsen leads the cast in Vinterberg's graduation film from the Danish National Film School. His character is a young man who is diagnosed with leukemia and given three months to live. He needs to decide how to say good-bye to his friends.

Drengen der gik baglæns (The Boy Who Walked Backwards; 1994, 37 min.)

Director, screenplay (chief writing credit to Bo hr. Hansen). Nine-year-old Andreas exhibits signs of obsessive-compulsive disorder after the death of his older brother in a motorcycle accident. With the alternative title *Tro, håb og Batman* (Faith, Hope and Batman), this short film represented Vinterberg's breakthrough and was awarded a ream of prizes: the Public Prize at Clemont-Ferrand in 1994, the best drama award at the 1995 Toronto Short Film Festival, and the best short film award and audience award at the 1994 Nordisk Panorama festival. Stylistically, the influence of Ingmar Bergman (especially *Fanny and Alexander* [1982]) is in evidence, though so too is there a dash of British "kitchen-sink" realism. The relationship between the brothers also has echoes of the later film *Submarino* (2010), while the party scenes are reminiscent of the dinner in *Festen*.

De største helte (The Greatest Heroes; 1996, 90 min.)

Director, screenplay (with Bo hr. Hansen). Vinterberg's first feature-length film is a road movie of sorts, bringing together the same ensemble of Ulrich Thomsen, Thomas Bo Larsen, Paprika Steen, Bjarne Henriksen, and Trine Dyrholm who would later underpin *Festen*. Larsen plays a newly released prisoner who discovers he has a twelve-year-old daughter. Together with his friend Peter (Thomsen) he whisks his daughter away from her unhappy home life, and they set off through Sweden with the aim of meeting up with two female friends, Pernille and Eva. The film won three prizes at the Danish Robert Festival.

Festen (The Celebration; 1998, 106 min.)

Director, screenplay (with Mogens Rukov). The first Dogma 95 film, and Vinterberg's international breakthrough. Its haul of awards included the Jury's Special Prize at Cannes in 1998, the Fassbinder Award at the European Film Awards of 1998, a double success as best foreign film in both the Los Angeles and New York Film Critics' Awards of 1998, and, not least, in Denmark, seven Robert prizes and three Bodil prizes.

Blur: No Distance Left to Run (1999, 6 min. approx.)

Not to be confused with Dylan Southern and Will Lovelace's 2010 documentary of the same name about the band Blur, Vinterberg's video films the BritPop four-piece while asleep, using night-vision goggles and helmet-mounted lamps. The song and accompanying nocturnal footage are bookended by sections in which the band, in split screen, explains the concept of the film and demonstrates the equipment and by a coda in which Vinterberg pulls open the curtains in the bedroom of the very groggy vocalist, Damon Albarn, to ask him what the song is about. The video features on the compilation DVD *The Best of Blur*, released by EMI in 2000.

D-Dag (D-Day; 2001, 70 min.)

Vinterberg was reunited with the other original Dogma 95 Brethren—Lars von Trier, Søren Kragh-Jacobsen, and Kristian Levring—to direct this experimental collective film shot during the New Year's Eve celebrations in Copenhagen at the turn of the year 2000. Four teams of actors (again including recognizable faces from the *Festen* stable) moved through the city, and the four Dogma brethren directed their movements in real time from a "control room." The resulting interdependent films were screened on New Year's Day 2000 across four television channels, allowing viewers to edit their own film by zapping between them with their remote controls. In 2001, a directors' cut of the material was released on DVD.

It's All about Love (2003, 104 min.)

Director and screenplay (with Mogens Rukov). Premiering in early January 2003, *It's All about Love* was Vinterberg's first English-language production, with an international cast headed by Claire Danes, Joaquin Phoenix, and Sean Penn. The film is set in New York in the near future, when people are dying in the street from broken hearts, sporadic gravitational failures oblige people to tether themselves to their houses and float helplessly, and the world is slowly coming to an end, smothered under a thick blanket of snow. Anthony Dod Mantle's cinematography has the luster and color palette of a Vermeer, but the special effects (cloned ice-skaters, floating villagers, freezing landscapes) gesture to a digital sublime. The film was not a success at the box office or with the critics, but it did win three prizes—for cinematography, special effects, and production design—at the 2004 Robert Festival in Copenhagen.

Dear Wendy (2005, 105 min.)

Director (screenplay by Lars von Trier). Another anglophone film, starring international actors Bill Pullman, Chris Owens, and Jamie Bell, and this time playing with the Western genre. Teenager Dick, who lives in a poor mining town in the American South, finds a pistol. He is a pacifist, but he is oddly fascinated and seduced by the weapon. He establishes a secret club in a disused mine where likeminded folk—the Dandies—can experiment in safety with their guns. They develop their own stylized shooting skills and refer to killing as "loving." Inevitably, their game spirals out of control and violently clashes with the real world. The film's voice-over is an extended letter from Dick to his beloved gun, Wendy, exploring the affinities between love and death. *Dear Wendy*'s themes and plot conceits can be seen as typical of von Trier's interest in analyzing U.S. culture and in blurring the boundaries between film and sociological experiment.

En mand kommer hjem (A Man Comes Home; 2007, 97 min.)

Director, screenplay (with Mogens Rukov and Morten Kaufmann). This film is a comedy, gently teasing the Danish audience with its propensity to reject native artists and others who make it big abroad. Thomas Bo Larsen is a renowned opera singer, returning to his hometown, while Oliver Møller Knauer is the lead character, Sebastian, a kitchen boy caught in a love triangle. The entanglement becomes even more complex when it is revealed that the opera singer may be Sebastian's father. The stately hotel setting allows for a recapitulation of *Festen*'s play with a complex space and story line and its upstairs-downstairs class dynamic. The star of the film, however, is probably the distinctive Danish summer daylight that brings the pale elegance of the set to life.

Metallica: The Day That Never Comes (2008, 9 min. approx.)

This music video was directed by Vinterberg to accompany the first single from Metallica's album *Death Magnetic* (2008). Widely available on YouTube and elsewhere, it depicts the life of a soldier in (presumably) Afghanistan, interspersed with footage of the band performing against the same mountainous backdrop. After a comrade is injured in a roadside detonation and airlifted to safety, bleeding heavily, the soldier continues his journey in an armored vehicle through the dusty landscape. The company happens upon a couple whose car seems to have broken down, but the two are assumed to be part of a trap until proven otherwise. In a tense standoff, the soldier finds himself eye to eye with the Afghan driver's veiled wife.

Submarino (2010, 110 min.)

Director, screenplay (with Tobias Lindholm). Though it has been critically acclaimed as a "return to form" for Vinterberg, *Submarino* breaks with his established practice in various ways. In part, this was prompted by a condition of co-funder TV-2, that half the cast and crew should be debutants. It is an adaptation of a novel by Jonas T. Bengtsson, with the screenplay cowritten with Lindholm; cinematographer Charlotte Bruus Christensen, shooting on 16mm, steps into the shoes of Vinterberg's longtime collaborator Anthony Dod Mantle. *Submarino* unveils the seamier side of life in Copenhagen, with freshman actors Jakob Cedergren and Peter Plaugborg taking on the roles of two brothers whose deprived childhood has sent them both spinning off the rails. Their parallel stories are told sequentially, driving home the sense of an inevitable descent into disaster. The film was awarded the Nordic Council's Film Prize of 2010.

Jagten (The Hunt; 2012, 115 min.)

Director, screenplay (with Tobias Lindholm). *Jagten* was the first Danish-language film since *Festen* to compete for the Palme d'Or at the 2012 Cannes Film Festival (though Lars von Trier's English-language *Dancer in the Dark* won in 2000). Starring Mads Mikkelsen, *Jagten* centers on a kindergarten teacher who becomes the victim of a witch hunt in a small Danish town. Charlotte Bruus Christensen again collaborates as cinematographer, this time shooting on digital (SxS PRO).

Notes

Introduction

1. This moment is documented in the film about the Dogma 95 movement, directed by Jesper Jargil: *De lutrede* [The Purified] (2002).
2. For a discussion of the immediate reaction in the Danish press, see Søren Kolstrup, "The Press and DOGMA 95," *P.O.V.*, no. 10 (2000), http://pov.imv.au.dk/Issue_10/section_4/artc3A.html.
3. I have chosen to use the Danish title *Festen* throughout this book, rather than the alternative English title *The Celebration*. Unusually, the Danish title was the one that was most widely used; even the posters advertising the play on Broadway adopted the Danish title.
4. *Morgenavisen Jyllands-Posten*, September 28, 1998. The first four Danish Dogma 95 films were shown on Danish television (Danmarks Radio) within three months of their theatrical release, which for *Festen* was June 19, 1998.
5. Ingmar Bergman, "Pure Kamikaze: Exclusive Ingmar Bergman Interview," by Stig Björkman, *Bergmanorama: The Magic Works of Ingmar Bergman*, http://bergmanorama.webs.com/films/saraband_sso2.htm, accessed January 10, 2012; originally published in *Sight and Sound*, September 2002, 14–15. Cage's inquiry was reported in Lis-

beth Jessen, *Efter "Festen"* [After *The Celebration*], radio montage, Danmarks Radio, P1, September 27, 2003, http://www.dr.dk/P1/Dokumentarzonen/Udsendelser/Montage/2003/10/10/000030.htm.

6   See, e.g., Donna Haraway, *When Species Meet* (Minneapolis: University of Minnesota Press, 2008), 31.

7   The Danish Ministry of Culture took down its online Danish Cultural Canon in 2012. A Danish version is currently available to download from http://kum.dk/Temaer/Temaarkiv/Kulturkanon (accessed January 6, 2013).

8   Lev Manovich bemoans the failure of turn-of-the-millennium theoreticians to construct a "genealogy for the language of computer media when it was just coming into being." Manovich's aim is to record and analyze the emerging language and practices of new media before they crystallize into convention and thus become invisible, as did the earliest iterations of cinema in the 1890s. Lev Manovich, introduction to *The Language of New Media* (Cambridge, Mass.: MIT Press, 2001), 7.

9   Mette Hjort and Scott MacKenzie, introduction to *Purity and Provocation: Dogma 95*, ed. Mette Hjort and Scott MacKenzie (London: British Film Institute, 2003), 13.

10 One exception is Palle Schantz Lauridsen's brief but detailed analysis in his essay "*The Celebration*: Classical Drama and Docu Soap Style," *P.O.V.*, no. 10 (2000), http://pov.imv.au.dk/Issue_10/section_3/artc1A.html.

11 Quoted in Mette Hjort and Ib Bondebjerg, eds., *The Danish Directors: Dialogues on a Contemporary National Cinema* (Bristol, U.K.: Intellect Books, 2000), 280–81.

12 For a detailed discussion of practitioners' agency within the framework of Dogma 95, see Mette Hjort, *Lone Scherfig's "Italian for Beginners,"* Nordic Film Classics (Seattle: University of Washington Press; Copenhagen: Museum Tusculanum Press, 2010), 40–99.

13 Brian Massumi, *Parables for the Virtual: Movement, Affect, Sensation* (Durham, N.C.: Duke University Press, 2002), 24–25.

14 Barbara M. Kennedy, *Deleuze and Cinema: The Aesthetics of Sensation* (Edinburgh: Edinburgh University Press, 2000), 48.
15 Massumi, *Parables for the Virtual*, 27.
16 Steven Shaviro, *Post-Cinematic Affect* (Winchester, U.K.: Zero Books, 2010), 6.
17 Manovich, *The Language of New Media*, 294.
18 Britta Timm Knudsen and Bodil Marie Thomsen, introduction to *Virkelighedshunger: Nyrealismen i visuel optik* [Reality-Hunger: New Realism in Visual Optics], ed. Britta Timm Knudsen and Bodil Marie Thomsen (Copenhagen: Tiderne Skifter, 2002), 10.

1. Dogma 95 and Danish Cinema

1 Philip French, "Spin Cycle: The Perils of Political Intrigue Are Examined in a Powerful Danish Thriller," *Observer*, September 25, 2005, http://www.guardian.co.uk/theobserver/2005/sep/25/features.review47.
2 David Bordwell, "A Strong Sense of Narrative Desire: A Decade of Danish Film," *FILM* (Magazine of the Danish Film Institute), no. 34 (2004): 24–27.
3 Mette Hjort, *Small Nation, Global Cinema: The New Danish Cinema* (Minneapolis: University of Minnesota Press, 2005).
4 "Generaldirektøren og den evige fred: Filmens forkyndelse af tanken om Europas forenede stater" [The Director General and Eternal Peace: Film's Promotion of the Concept of a United States of Europe], *Berlingske Tidende*, July 14, 1917, Danish Film Institute archive, Copenhagen.
5 For an illustrated history of Danish cinema in English, see the Danish Film Institute's online *Danish Film History* by Peter Schepelern: http://www.dfi.dk/English/Danish-Film-History.aspx.
6 Hjort, *Small Nation, Global Cinema*, 5.
7 Ibid., 12–14.
8 Ibid., 5–8.

9 Ibid., 9.
10 See Peter Schepelern, "Filmen ifølge Dogme: Spilleregler, forhindringer og befrielser" [Film according to Dogma: Ground Rules, Obstacles, and Liberations], *Nationale spejlinger: Tendenser i ny dansk film* [National Reflections: Tendencies in New Danish Cinema], ed. Anders Toftgaard and Ian Hawkesworth (Copenhagen: Museum Tusculanum Press, 2003), 74–75.
11 *Trier on von Trier*, ed. Stig Björkman, trans. Neil Smith (London: Faber and Faber, 2003), 202.
12 Kolstrup, "The Press and DOGMA 95."
13 Hjort and MacKenzie, introduction to *Purity and Provocation*, 3.
14 Schepelern, "Filmen ifølge Dogme," 75.
15 Lars von Trier, "Project 'Open Film Town,'" in Hjort and Bondebjerg, *The Danish Directors*, 225.
16 Ibid., 226.
17 The quotations that follow are taken from the Zentropa Post Production Hotel's official web pages at http://www.zpp.dk (accessed January 11, 2011; now defunct). As of December 2012, the facility is referred to as Klippegangen on Zentropa's website: www.zentropa.dk/about/facilities/klippegangen.
18 Quoted in Hjort and Bondebjerg, *The Danish Directors*, 277.
19 Marcus Aggersbjerg, *Rukov—et portræt* [Rukov—a Portrait] (Copenhagen: People's Press, 2010).
20 "Det smukkeste er hengivelsen: Interview med Mogens Rukov" [The Most Beautiful Thing Is Surrender: Interview with Mogens Rukov], by Nikolaj Mangurten Lassen, *Weekendavisen*, September 9, 2010, http://www.weekendavisen.dk/.
21 Ibid. Unless otherwise indicated, translations from Danish sources are my own.
22 Dogme95 FAQs, http://web.archive.org/web/20080420163820/www.dogme95.dk/menu/menuset.htm, accessed January 8, 2011. The Dogme95 website, now defunct, has been archived by the Internet Archive, whose URL is provided here.

23 Richard Kelly, *The Name of This Book Is Dogme95* (London: Faber and Faber, 2000), 117.
24 Hjort, *Small Nation, Global Cinema*, 37–42, 39.
25 Erik Skyum-Nielsen, *Engle i sneen: Lyrik og prosa i 90erne* [Angels in the Snow: Poetry and Prose in the 1990s] (Copenhagen: Gyldendal, 2000).
26 See, e.g., Søren Mørch, *Den sidste Danmarkshistorie* [The Last History of Denmark] (Copenhagen: Gad, 1996).
27 The Danish research project "Realitet, realisme, det reelle i visuel optik" [Reality, Realism, and the Real in Visual Culture] resulted in three edited anthologies between 2002 and 2005: Knudsen and Thomsen, *Virkelighedshunger*; *Virkelighed! Virkelighed! Avantgardens realisme* [Reality! Reality! The Realism of the Avant-Garde], ed. Mette Sandbye (Copenhagen: Tiderne Skifter, 2003); and the English-language *Performative Realism: Interdisciplinary Studies in Art and Media*, ed. Rune Gade and Anne Jerslev (Copenhagen: Museum Tusculanum Press, 2005).
28 Knudsen and Thomsen, introduction to *Virkelighedshunger*, 7.
29 Ibid., 10.
30 Bodil Marie Thomsen, "Sansernes realisme—om etik, rum og begivenhed i Lars von Triers 90'er-trilogi" [Realism of the Senses—on Ethics, Space, and Event in Lars von Trier's 1990s Trilogy], in Knudsen and Thomsen, *Virkelighedshunger*, 123–24.
31 Hjort and Bondebjerg, *The Danish Directors*, 280.
32 Jack Stevenson, *Dogme Uncut: Lars von Trier, Thomas Vinterberg, and the Gang That Took on Hollywood* (Santa Monica, Calif.: Santa Monica Press, 2003), 84–85.
33 I am alluding here to Paul Connerton's argument that collective memory functions on two levels: inscribed (in written records or other forms of recorded data) and incorporated (learned bodily practices). Paul Connerton, *How Societies Remember* (Cambridge: Cambridge University Press, 1989).
34 Kelly, *The Name of This Book Is Dogme95*, 117.

35 For an account of current thought on the distinction between (preconscious) affect and (conscious) emotion, see Shaviro, *Post-Cinematic Affect*, especially 3–6. Jack Stevenson reports in *Dogme Uncut* (86) that many reviewers critiqued Gbatokai as "flat" or "thrown in."

36 For an account of the history of this project, see Rune Engelbreth Larsen, "Støtteerklæring til Zentropas Dannebrog-initiativet" [Declaration of Support for Zentropa's Danish Flag Initiative], Humanisme.dk, June 5, 2004, http://www.humanisme.dk/debat/debat134.php. For a longer commentary, see C. Claire Thomson, "Cultivate the Nation, Don't Nationalise Culture! Intercultural Cinema in a Small Language Department," Liaison Magazine (*LLAS Subject Centre*), no. 4 (2010), http://www.llas.ac.uk/resourcedownloads/179/liaison_jan10.pdf.

2. The Auteur and Cinema History

1. Mogens Rukov, "Adventures of a Productive Idiot," *Guardian*, October 26, 2002, Saturday section, 17.
2. Hjort, *Small Nation, Global Cinema*, 42–43.
3. See, e.g., the seminal essay by Tom Gunning, "Now You See It, Now You Don't: The Temporality of the Cinema of Attractions," in *The Silent Cinema Reader*, ed. Lee Grieveson and Peter Krämer (London: Routledge, 2004), 41–50; and the anthology *The Cinema of Attractions Reloaded*, ed. Wanda Strauven (Amsterdam: Amsterdam University Press, 2006).
4. Manovich, *The Language of New Media*, 288.
5. Ibid., 308.
6. Ibid., 294–95.
7. Ian Conrich and Estella Tincknell, "Film Purity, the Neo-Bazinian Ideal, and Humanism in Dogma 95," *P.O.V.*, no. 10 (2000), http://pov.imv.au.dk/Issue_10/section_4/artc7A.html.
8. Paprika Steen, for example, who plays Helene, tells Richard Kelly in an interview: "I found I'd be peering about me, trying to get my

bearings, thinking, 'Where is the camera? There? Or there?' I know that in the editing they had to lose so many shots where I just look straight in the camera." Quoted in Kelly, *The Name of This Book Is Dogme95*, 165–66. For an account of responses to the camera in early cinema, see Jonathan Auerbach, *Body Shots: Early Cinema's Incarnations* (Berkeley: University of California Press, 2008).

9   Bodil Marie Thomsen has pointed out that this phrase might also be referring to the ending of Godard's *King Lear* (1987), in which an encounter with Woody Allen ends the film—together with almost the same words about ripples on a shore. See Bodil Marie Thomsen, "Lear—liar—real: Om Jean-Luc Godards *King Lear* og Kristian Levrings *The King Is Alive*" [Lear—Liar—Real: On Jean-Luc Godard's *King Lear* and Kristian Levring's *The King Is Alive*], in *Om som om: Antologi om realisme* [On "As If": An Anthology about Realism], ed. Stefan Iversen, Heidi Jørgensen, and Henrik Skov Nielsen, 148–67 (Copenhagen: Akademisk Forlag, 2002).

10 Dogme95 FAQs, archived at http://web.archive.org/web/20080420163820/www.dogme95.dk/menu/menuset.htm.

11 Quoted in Hjort and Bondebjerg, *The Danish Directors*, 221.

12 Dogme95 FAQs, archived as above.

13 "Celebrating Limitations: An Interview with Thomas Vinterberg," by Bo Green Jensen, *Weekendavisen*, April 1998, archived at http://web.archive.org/web/20070708192051/www.dogme95.dk/celebration/index.htm.

14 Roland Barthes, "From Work to Text," in *Image—Music—Text*, essays selected and trans. Stephen Heath (London: Fontana, 1977), 155–64, 160.

15 Berys Gaut, "Naked Film: Dogma and Its Limits," in Hjort and MacKenzie, *Purity and Provocation*, 92.

16 Hjort, *Lone Scherfig's "Italian for Beginners,"* 40–99.

17 Thomas Vinterberg and Mogens Rukov, "Mere end én gang tænkte vi på Hamlet" [More than Once We Thought of Hamlet], in *Festen og andre skandaler: Udvalgte artikler 1992–2002* [*The Celebration* and

Other Scandals: Selected Writings, 1992–2002], by Mogens Rukov, ed. Claus Christensen (Copenhagen: Lindhardt Ringhof, 2002), 75–80, 78.

18 "På en eller anden måde tilhører filmen instruktøren. Allerede i manuskriptet." Ibid.

19 Linda Haverty Rugg, "Globalization and the Auteur: Ingmar Bergman Projected Internationally," in *Transnational Cinema in a Global North: Nordic Cinema in Transition*, ed. Andrew Nestingen and Trevor Elkington (Detroit: Wayne State University Press, 2005), 221–41.

20 Thomas Vinterberg, interview by Anne Mette Traberg Jørgensen, Copenhagen, August 2007, unpublished; Danish transcript in the author's possession.

21 Hjort, *Small Nation, Global Cinema*, 187.

22 For a more thorough discussion of this film, see C. Claire Thomson, "It's All about Snow: Limning the Posthuman Body in Соляpис/ *Solaris* (Tarkovsky, 1972) and *It's All about Love* (Vinterberg, 2003)," *New Cinemas: Journal of Contemporary Film* 5, no. 1 (2007): 3–21.

23 Bo Green Jensen, "Interview: Premiere; Manden, der gik baglæns" [Interview: Premiere; The Man Who Walked Backwards] (includes an interview with Thomas Vinterberg), and "Redux: En lille film on nåde" [Redux: A Little Film about Grace], both in *Weekendavisen*, March 26, 2010, http://www.weekendavisen.dk/.

24 Danish Film Institute, "Vinterberg til Cannes Festival" [Vinterberg to Cannes Festival], April 19, 2012, http://www.dfi.dk/Nyheder/Nyheder-FraDFI/2012/Vinterberg-til-Cannes-Festival.aspx.

25 Green Jensen, "The Man Who Walked Backwards."

3. Dogma 95 and the Death of Film

Epigraphs: Jeremy Lehrer, "Denmark's DV Director Thomas Vinterberg Delves into *The Celebration*" (includes an interview with

Thomas Vinterberg), *indieWIRE*, October 14, 1998, http://www.indiewire.com/article/denmarks_dv_director_thomas_vinterberg_delves_into_the_celebration; Svetlana Boym, "The Off-Modern Mirror," *e-flux*, no. 19 (2010), http://www.e-flux.com/journal/the-off-modern-mirror.

1. Laura Mulvey, *Death 24x a Second: Stillness and the Moving Image* (London: Reaktion Books, 2006), 181.
2. Ibid., 17.
3. "A Reader's Report to the Publisher," in *The Death of Cinema: History, Cultural Memory, and the Digital Dark Age*, by Paolo Cherchi Usai (London: British Film Institute, 2001), 111–27.
4. Mulvey, *Death 24x a Second*, 18.
5. James Monaco, *How to Read a Film: Movies, Media, and Beyond* (Oxford: Oxford University Press, 2009), 667.
6. David Ehrenstein, "Film in the Age of Video: 'Oh, We Don't Know Where We're Going But We're on Our Way,'" *Film Quarterly* 49, no. 3 (1996): 40.
7. David Rodowick, *The Virtual Life of Film* (Cambridge, Mass.: Harvard University Press, 2007), 7; Monaco, *How to Read a Film*, 144. The first digitally edited film to receive an Academy Award for editing was *The English Patient*, the Oscar going to editor Walter Murch in 1996—the same year Thomas Vinterberg conceived the story line for *Festen*. See IMDb, *The English Patient* (1996), "Trivia," http://www.imdb.com/title/tt0116209/trivia, accessed January 13, 2012.
8. "En vidunderlig smidig elektronisk billedskrivemaskine, en Awid." Vinterberg and Rukov, "More than Once We Thought of Hamlet," 77.
9. Mulvey, *Death 24x a Second*, 27.
10. Ibid.
11. Shaviro, *Post-Cinematic Affect*, 2.
12. Ibid., 133–34.
13. Rodowick, *The Virtual Life of Film*, 3.
14. Ibid., 4.
15. Ibid., 5.

16 Stephen Prince, "True Lies: Perceptual Realism, Digital Images, and Film Theory," *Film Quarterly* 49, no. 3 (1996): 27–37.
17 Manovich, *The Language of New Media*, 300–301.
18 Ibid., 293–308.
19 Schepelern, "Filmen ifølge Dogme," 62.
20 Kelly, *The Name of This Book Is Dogme95*, 100; see also Dogme95 FAQs, http://web.archive.org/web/20070708192230/www.dogme95.dk/menu/menuset.htm, accessed January 15, 2011.
21 Rodowick, *The Virtual Life of Film*, 8. In contrast, Monaco, in *How to Read a Film* (671), identifies Mike Figgis's *Timecode* (2000) as "the first all-digital production." The discrepancy here may be attributed to the interpretation of "commercial."
22 Dogme95 FAQs, http://web.archive.org/web/20080420163820/www.dogme95.dk/menu/menuset.htm, accessed January 15, 2011.
23 Ibid.
24 Manovich reports that less than 17 percent of content on YouTube in early 2010 was user generated. Lev Manovich (blog), "The Myth of User-Generated Content," November 23, 2010, http://manovich.net/, accessed March 15, 2012.
25 Dogme95 FAQs, http://web.archive.org/web/20080420163820/www.dogme95.dk/menu/menuset.htm. The same web page goes on to explain a practical consideration rooted in the incompatibility of the respective typical aspect ratios of DV cameras and theatrical screens: "Your photographer has to remember that the DV film has to be transferred to 35mm Academy, which is the almost square, old film format 1.33:1. So be sure that there is no confusion at all regarding what you have in your viewfinder and what comes on to the 35mm print."
26 Svetlana Boym, *The Future of Nostalgia* (New York: Basic Books, 2001), xiii.
27 Ibid., xiv.
28 Svetlana Boym, "Nostalgic Technology: Notes for an Off-Modern Manifesto," n.d., *Svetlana Boym | Media Art*, http://www.svetla-

naboym.com/manifesto.htm, accessed March 27, 2012.
29 See, e.g., Emily Eakin, "Celluloid Hero," *New Yorker*, October 31, 2011, 54; and Adrian Searle, "Tacita Dean: *Film*—Review," *Guardian*, October 10, 2011, http://www.guardian.co.uk/artanddesign/2011/oct/10/tacita-dean-film-review.
30 Tacita Dean, "Save Celluloid, for Art's Sake," *Guardian*, February 22, 2011, http://www.guardian.co.uk/artanddesign/2011/feb/22/tacita-dean-16mm-film.
31 *FILM: Tacita Dean*, ed. Nicholas Cullinan, Unilever Series (London: Tate Publishing, 2011).
32 Dean, "Save Celluloid."
33 Manovich, *The Language of New Media*, 294–95.
34 Ibid., 294.
35 For an account of video as an intermediate technology and medium between analogue film and digital, see Yvonne Spielmann, *Video: The Reflexive Medium*, trans. Anja Welle and Stan Jones (Cambridge, Mass.: MIT Press, 2008).
36 Jean Baudrillard, *The Illusion of the End*, trans. Chris Turner (Stanford, Calif.: Stanford University Press, 1994), 55.
37 André Bazin, "The Ontology of the Photographic Image," in *What Is Cinema?*, essays selected and trans. Hugh Gray (Berkeley: University of California Press, 2005), 1:9.
38 Roland Barthes, *Camera Lucida: Reflections on Photography*, trans. Richard Howard (London: Vintage, 1993), 80–81.
39 Bazin, "The Ontology of the Photographic Image," 14, 15.
40 Ibid., 12n.
41 Rodowick, *The Virtual Life of Film*, 123.
42 Ibid., 117–21.
43 Laura U. Marks, "How Electrons Remember," in *Touch: Sensuous Theory and Multisensory Media* (Minneapolis: University of Minnesota Press, 2002), 161–76.
44 Mulvey, *Death 24x a Second*, 22.
45 Ibid., 66.

46 Quoted in Lehrer, "Denmark's DV Director" (brackets in the original).
47 Manovich, *The Language of New Media*, 293.
48 Ibid., 294–95.
49 Shaviro, *Post-Cinematic Affect*, 133.
50 Boym, "The Off-Modern Mirror."

4. The Handheld Camera

Epigraph: Ingmar Bergman, "Pure Kamikaze," 15.

1 Peter Matthews, review of *Festen*, directed by Thomas Vinterberg, *Sight and Sound*, March 1999, http://old.bfi.org.uk/sightandsound/review/49.
2 James Monaco, *The Dictionary of New Media: The New Digital World of Video, Audio, and Print* (New York: Harbor Electronic Publishers, 2007), 38.
3 Wheeler Winston Dixon dates Godard's first experiments with the Portapak to early 1969. Wheeler Winston Dixon, *The Films of Jean-Luc Godard* (Albany: State University of New York Press, 1997), 110.
4 For an overview of Farocki's career with handheld and video cameras, see Thomas Elsaesser, ed., *Harun Farocki: Working on the Sight-Lines* (Amsterdam: Amsterdam University Press, 2004); and Harun Farocki's website, http://www.farocki-film.de.
5 Quoted in Chris Meigh-Andrews, *A History of Video Art: The Development of Form and Function* (Oxford, U.K.: Berg, 2006), 8.
6 Quoted in Kelly, *The Name of This Book Is Dogme95*, 101.
7 Ibid., 100 (emphasis added). See also Lehrer, "Denmark's DV Director," in which Vinterberg compares the cameras in size to a coffee mug and to the journalist's tape recorder.
8 "Og jeg kan huske, at, jeg springer lige tilbage til min midtvejsfilm, Brudevalsen hed den, der skulle vi lave 15 mins film på meget kort tid. På filmskolen. Så tog jeg den af fotograferne der gik til tai chi, og kunne holde et kamera mindst stille, og så smed jeg alt kameraudstyret væk

og sagde vi laver den her film håndholdt. Og det var der sgu ikke nogen der havde gjort herhjemme før. Og det var den Trier havde set. Det var min midtvejsfilm han havde set da han spurgte mig om at lave dogme." Vinterberg, interview by Traberg Jørgensen.

9   See, e.g., Peter Schepelern, "Film according to Dogma: Ground Rules, Obstacles, and Liberations," in Nestingen and Elkington, *Transnational Cinema in a Global North*, 80–81; Vinterberg, interview by Traberg Jørgensen; and Stevenson, *Dogme Uncut*, 25–36. Paprika Steen, too, mentions that her favorite actress is Gena Rowlands, wife of Cassavetes (Kelly, *The Name of This Book Is Dogme95*, 165).

10 Angelos Koutsourakis, "John Cassavetes: The First Dogme Director?," Bright Lights Film Journal, no. 63 (2009), http://www.brightlightsfilm.com/63/63cassavetes.php.

11 Quoted in Kelly, *The Name of This Book Is Dogme95*, 117.

12 Ibid., 166.

13 Ibid., 101.

14 For a sustained discussion of the tension between fiction and reality in *The Idiots*, see Anne Jerslev, "Dogma 95, Lars von Trier's *The Idiots*, and the "Idiot Project," in *Realism and "Reality" in Film and Media*, ed. Anne Jerslev (Copenhagen: Museum Tusculanum Press, 2002), 41–65.

15 Todd Berliner, "Hollywood Movie Dialogue and the 'Real Realism' of John Cassavetes," *Film Quarterly* 52, no. 3 (1999): 9.

16 *Cassavetes on Cassavetes*, ed. Raymond Carney (London: Faber and Faber, 2001), 72.

17 George Kouvaros, "Where Does It Happen? The Place of Performance in the Work of John Cassavetes," *Screen* 39, no. 3 (1998): 251.

18 Gilles Deleuze, *Cinema 1: The Movement-Image*, trans. Hugh Tomlinson and Barbara Habberjam (London: Continuum, 1986), 89.

19 Knudsen and Thomsen, introduction to *Virkelighedshunger*, 8.

20 Deleuze, *Cinema 1*, 89.

21 Quoted in Mark Monahan, "Film-Makers on Film: Thomas Vinterberg; Thomas Vinterberg Talks to Mark Monahan about Andrei Tar-

kovsky's *Stalker* (1979)," *Telegraph*, February 16, 2004, http://www.telegraph.co.uk/culture/film/3612441/Film-makers-on-film-Thomas-Vinterberg.html.
22 Kouvaros, "Where Does It Happen?," 251.
23 Schepelern, "Film according to Dogma," 87.
24 *Cassavetes on Cassavetes*, 72.
25 Matthews, review of *Festen*.
26 Kouvaros, "Where Does It Happen?," 254–55.
27 Ibid., 258.
28 Kelly, *The Name of This Book Is Dogme95*, 101.
29 I am alluding here to Giuliana Bruno's splicing of motion and emotion in her book *Atlas of Emotion: Journeys in Art, Architecture, and Film* (London: Verso, 2002); see especially 250–51.
30 This scene is mentioned as an instance of improvisation in Vinterberg and Rukov, "More than Once We Thought of Hamlet," 82.
31 Berliner, "Hollywood Movie Dialogue," 9.

5. The Hotel

Epigraph: Giuliana Bruno, *Atlas of Emotion*, 58.
1 Ellen Rees, "In My Father's House Are Many Mansions: Transgressive Space in Three Dogma 95 Films," *Scandinavica* 43, no. 2 (2004): 165–82.
2 Skjoldenæsholm's web pages can be found at http://www.skj.dk.
3 Danish Ministry of Culture, *1001 Stories of Denmark*, http://www.kulturarv.dk/1001fortaellinger/en_GB/skjoldenaesholm, accessed January 15, 2011.
4 Michel Foucault, "Different Spaces," in *Essential Works of Foucault, 1954–1984*, vol. 2, *Aesthetics, Method, and Epistemology*, ed. James D. Faubion, trans. Robert Hurley et al. (London: Penguin, 1998), 175–86. The concept of *heterotopia* was first promulgated in a speech, "Des espaces autres," given in 1967, but not approved for publication in French until 1984, and translated for the journal *Diacritics* two years later as "Of Other Spaces."

5   "Hvor svundne tiders stemning og nutidig komfort forenes." Skjoldenæsholm, "Historie," http://www.skj.dk/Default.asp?ID=211, accessed January 15, 2011.
6   Marc Augé, *Non-places: Introduction to the Anthropology of Supermodernity*, trans. John Howe (London: Verso, 1995).
7   Bruno, *Atlas of Emotion*, 56. Bruno is discussing Sergei Eisenstein's essay "Montage and Architecture," which dates from ca. 1938 and was published in *Assemblage*, no. 10 (1989): 111–31.
8   Manovich, *The Language of New Media*, 107.
9   Ibid., 113.
10 Bruno, *Atlas of Emotion*, 60–61.
11 Skjoldenæsholm, "Parken," http://www.skj.dk/Default.asp?ID=213, accessed January 15, 2011.
12 Bruno, *Atlas of Emotion*, 61.
13 Ibid., 56.
14 Ibid.
15 Manovich, *The Language of New Media*, 293–300. For a longer discussion of this point, see Thomson, "It's All about Snow."
16 For a brief history of the tapestries, and an image of one of them, see Skjoldenæsholm, "Om Skjoldenæsholm," http://www.skj.dk/Default.asp?ID=210, accessed January 28, 2011.
17 Bruno, *Atlas of Emotion*, especially 171–84.

6. Sense Memory and the Haptic

Epigraph: Giuliana Bruno, *Atlas of Emotion*, 66.

1   "En ulækkers glas": mistranslated in the subtitles of the 2002 Bluelight edition as "Just don't use someone's dirty glass."
2   *Festen*, directed by Thomas Vinterberg (London: Bluelight, 2002), DVD.
3   Laura U. Marks, *The Skin of the Film: Intercultural Cinema, Embodiment, and the Senses* (Durham, N.C.: Duke University Press, 2000), 97–114, 96.

4   Ibid., 192.
5   Jennifer M. Barker, *The Tactile Eye: Touch and the Cinematic Experience* (Berkeley: University of California Press, 2009), 38.
6   Marks, *The Skin of the Film*, 132.
7   I am thinking here of Isak Dinesen's tale "The Blank Page," in *Last Tales* (New York: Random House, 1957), 99–105.
8   Vinterberg describes this as a "cynical theft" from Bergman's *Fanny och Alexander* [Fanny and Alexander; 1982], and Visconti's *Il Gattopardo* [The Leopard; 1963]. Quoted in Hjort and Bondebjerg, *The Danish Directors*, 181.
9   Laura U. Marks, "Thinking Multisensory Culture," *Paragraph* 31, no. 2 (2008): 126.
10 Eleanor Margolies, "Vagueness Gridlocked: A Map of the Smells of New York," in *The Smell Culture Reader*, ed. Jim Drobnick (Oxford, U.K.: Berg, 2005), 111.
11 Marks, *Touch: Sensuous Theory and Multisensory Media*, 119.
12 For an expanded version of this discussion about smell in cinema in the context of a Norwegian short film, see C. Claire Thomson, "Air, Scent, and the Senses: Unni Straume's *Derailment*," *Short Film Studies* 1, no. 2 (2011): 245–49.
13 Lehrer, "Denmark's DV Director."
14 Kelly, *The Name of This Book Is Dogme95*, 100.
15 Ibid., 101–2.
16 Dogma95, FAQs on Dogme #1, *Festen* [The Celebration], archived at http://web.archive.org/web/20080420163820/www.dogme95.dk/menu/menuset.htm, accessed January 15, 2011.
17 A. L. Rees, *A History of Experimental Film and Video* (London: British Film Institute, 1999), 113.
18 Meigh-Andrews, *A History of Video Art*, 262.
19 Rodowick, *The Virtual Life of Film*, 120.
20 Laura U. Marks, "Loving a Disappearing Image," in *Touch: Sensuous Theory and Multisensory Media*, 91.

7. The Story of Allan

Epigraph: Mogens Rukov, "Adventures of a Productive Idiot," 17.

1. Jack Stevenson also gives an account of Allan's story, and the ensuing investigations, in *Dogme Uncut*, 88–91.
2. "Ti år med Koplevs Krydsfelt" [Ten Years with *Koplev's Crossword*], *Information*, December 30, 2003, http://www.information.dk/89119; Kjeld Koplev, "Læserbreve: Koplevs køkken" [Readers' Letters: Koplev's Kitchen], *Information*, August 16, 2006, http://www.information.dk/127934.
3. Jessen, *After "The Celebration."*
4. Rukov, "Adventures of a Productive Idiot," 17.
5. Claus Christensen, "Festen der forsvandt" [The Party That Disappeared], *Weekendavisen*, April 5, 2000, http://www.weekendavisen.dk/.
6. Ibid.
7. Claus Christensen, "Stadig tvivl om Festen" [There's Still Doubt about *The Celebration*], *Weekendavisen*, June 22, 2000, http://www.weekendavisen.dk/.
8. Ibid.
9. Jessen, *After "The Celebration."*
10. "Interview: Lisbeth Jessen," by Birgitte Hornhaver, *Dokumentarzonen* [Documentary Zone], broadcast August 8, 2007, 14:00, Danmarks Radio P1, http://www.dr.dk/P1/Dokumentarzonen/Udsendelser/2007/08/11082855.htm.
11. Ibid.
12. Schepelern, "Film according to Dogme," 86.
13. Jessen, "Interview."
14. Jessen, *After "The Celebration."*
15. Jessen, "Interview."
16. Claus Christensen, "Der var engang en fest" [Once Upon a Time There Was a Party], *Filmmagasinet Ekko*, no. 18 (2003), http://www.ekkofilm.dk/essays.asp?table=essays&id=19.

17 "Every man-made object, including drama, has its own archaeology," begins Rukov, in "Adventures of a Productive Idiot" (17).
18 Jessen, After *"The Celebration."*
19 A final layer of intertextuality is provided by a "lost" film from 1994 in which a tuxedo-clad Ulrich Thomsen rehearses a speech to his estranged father. The film in question was an advertisement for Danish State Railways, directed by the Norwegian Hans Petter Moland, and has been acknowledged by Vinterberg as an incidental source of inspiration for the staging of Christian's speech in *Festen*. Claus Christensen, "Reklamefilm åbnede *Festen*" [Advertisement Got *The Celebration* Started], *Filmmagasinet Ekko*, August 28, 2003, http://www.ekkofilm.dk/?allowbreak=false&id=28. Many thanks to Mette Hjort for bringing this source to my attention.
20 Rukov, "The Most Beautiful Thing Is Surrender."

8. *Festen* from Screen to Stage

Epigraph: André Bazin, "Theater and Cinema: Part Two," in *What Is Cinema?*, 1:105–6.
1 David Benedict, "West End Ready for Its Closeup," *Variety*, August 27, 2007, 117.
2 Ibid.
3 Quoted in ibid.
4 Unfortunately, the Almeida Theatre was unable to assist with material for this project. However, it is likely that visual and written material on *Festen* will, in due course, be added to the theater's online archive, at http://www.almeida.co.uk/about-us/archive.
5 Heidi Amsinck, "Nyt liv med *Festen*" [New Life for *The Celebration*], *Morgenavisen Jyllands-Posten*, February 2, 2005, clippings folder, Danish Film Institute archive, Copenhagen.
6 *Politiken*, February 11, 2006, clippings folder, Danish Film Institute archive, Copenhagen.
7 Tina Gylling Mortensen, Claus Flygare, and Thomas Bendixen,

"Debat: Åbent brev fra Mammutteatret" [Debate: Open Letter from Mammoth Theatre Company], *Information*, August 18, 2006, 32–33; Gasværket Teater, "Pressemeddelelse: Thomas Vinterbergs *Festen*" [Press Release: Thomas Vinterberg's *The Celebration*], October 2007, http://www.gasvaerket.dk/.

8   In the English-language collection of Bazin's writings *What Is Cinema?*, fully two essays on "theater and cinema" survived the editing process from the original four-volume French anthology of his writings.

9   Bazin, "Theater and Cinema: Part Two," 97–98.

10 Bo hr. Hansen, e-mail communication with Peter Schepelern, March 11, 2011. I am grateful to Bo hr. Hansen and Peter Schepelern for clarifying this point.

11 Rukov, "Adventures of a Productive Idiot," 17.

12 I base this observation on the Danish and French versions of the text by Vinterberg, Rukov, and Hansen; the French text was translated by Daniel Benoin, with the assistance of Sejer Andersen.

13 Again, Bo hr. Hansen has clarified (in a personal communication with Peter Schepelern) that he produced two versions of the original Danish play: one with a limited number of characters and one with a more extensive cast. The option to have a larger cast was used by Mammutteatret, the first Danish theater company to stage the play.

14 Rebecca Manson Jones and Sarah Dickenson, *Festen: Projects Pack* (London: Almeida Projects, 2006), 14, http://www.almeida.co.uk/Downloads/development/resources/FestenTourProjectsPack.pdf.

15 Alex Sierz, "In Britain, the Writer Is King," *Financial Times*, March 17, 2004, London edition, 15. See also Jones and Dickenson, *Festen: Projects Pack*, 13.

16 Jones and Dickenson, *Festen: Projects Pack*, 11.

17 Ibid., 13.

18 Rukov, "Adventures of a Productive Idiot," 17.

19 Many thanks to Geraldine Brodie for drawing the affinity with Pinter to my attention, and for her thoughtful comments on this chapter.

20. David Eldridge, *Festen*, Modern Plays (London: Methuen Drama, 2004), 44.
21. Jones and Dickenson, *Festen: Projects Pack*, 11.
22. Sarah Hemming, review of *Festen*, adapted by David Eldridge, directed by Rufus Norris, Almeida Theatre, London, *Financial Times*, March 29, 2004, London edition 1, Arts section, 17.
23. Jones and Dickenson, *Festen: Projects Pack*, 7.
24. Lauridsen, "*The Celebration*: Classical Drama and Docu Soap Style."
25. Jesper Thobo-Carlsen, "*Festen* udeblev på Broadway" [*The Celebration* Out of It on Broadway], *Berlingske Tidende*, April 12, 2006, clippings folder, Danish Film Institute archive, Copenhagen.
26. "*Festen* er forbi på Broadway" [*The Celebration* Is Over on Broadway], *B.T.*, May 17, 2006, Danish Film Institute archive, Copenhagen.
27. Thobo-Carlsen, "*The Celebration* Out of It on Broadway."
28. This production ran November 9–19, 2011, at the Pit Theatre in London's Barbican complex.
29. Quoted in Green Jensen, "The Man Who Walked Backwards."
30. Ibid.

9. Media and Time

Epigraph: Laura U. Marks, "Loving a Disappearing Image," *Cinémas: Revue d'études cinématographiques / Cinémas: Journal of Film Studies* 8, nos. 1–2 (1997): 97.

1. The essay was republished as part of the anthology of Marks's essays titled *Touch: Sensuous Theory and Multisensory Media*, put out by the University of Minnesota Press in 2002.
2. Rodowick, *The Virtual Life of Film*, 26.
3. Marks, "Loving a Disappearing Image" (1997), 96.
4. Schepelern, "Film according to Dogma," 87.
5. Rukov, "Adventures of a Productive Idiot," 17.

6   Vinterberg and Rukov, "More than Once We Thought of Hamlet," 78–79.
7   Vilhelm Hammershøi (1864–1916) was a Danish painter best known for studies of interior architecture and space. His influence on the Danish filmmaker Carl Th. Dreyer is examined in detail in Anne-Birgitte Fonsmark, ed., *Hammershøi > Dreyer: The Magic of Images* (Copenhagen: Ordrupgaard Museum, 2006).
8   Rebecca Harrison, "Haunted Screens and Spiritual Scenes: Film as a Medium in the Cinema of Carl Theodor Dreyer," *Scandinavica* 48, no. 1 (2009): 41.
9   Barthes, *Camera Lucida*, 38.
10 Mulvey, *Death 24x a Second*, 181.
11 The clip was presented as part of the multimedia Cultural Canon website at http://kulturkanon.kum.dk/film/festen/Se-klip (last accessed July 26, 2012). The Canon's homepage was closed in September 2012; a Danish version of the text and still images in portable document format can currently be downloaded from http://kum.dk/Temaer/Temaarkiv/Kulturkanon/ (accessed January 7, 2013).
12 Mulvey, *Death 24x a Second*, 66.
13 Ibid., 193.

Bibliography

Aggersbjerg, Marcus. *Rukov—et portræt* [Rukov—a Portrait]. Copenhagen: People's Press, 2010.
Amsinck, Heidi. "Nyt liv med *Festen*" [New Life for *The Celebration*]. *Morgenavisen Jyllands-Posten*, February 2, 2005. Clippings folder, Danish Film Institute archive, Copenhagen.
Auerbach, Jonathan. *Body Shots: Early Cinema's Incarnations*. Berkeley: University of California Press, 2008.
Augé, Marc. *Non-places: Introduction to the Anthropology of Supermodernity*. Translated by John Howe. London: Verso, 1995.
Barker, Jennifer M. *The Tactile Eye: Touch and the Cinematic Experience*. Berkeley: University of California Press, 2009.
Barthes, Roland. *Camera Lucida: Reflections on Photography*. Translated by Richard Howard. London: Vintage, 1993.
———. "From Work to Text." In *Image—Music—Text*. Essays selected and translated by Stephen Heath, 155–64. London: Fontana, 1977.
Baudrillard, Jean. *The Illusion of the End*. Translated by Chris Turner. Stanford, Calif.: Stanford University Press, 1994.
Bazin, André. *What Is Cinema?* Vol. 1. Essays selected and translated by Hugh Gray. Berkeley: University of California Press, 2005.

Benedict, David. "West End Ready for Its Closeup." *Variety*, August 27, 2007, 117.

Bergman, Ingmar. "Pure Kamikaze: Exclusive Ingmar Bergman Interview." By Stig Björkman. *Bergmanorama: The Magic Works of Ingmar Bergman*. http://bergmanorama.webs.com/films/saraband_ss02.htm. Accessed January 10, 2012. Originally published in *Sight and Sound*, September 2002, 14–15.

Berliner, Todd. "Hollywood Movie Dialogue and the 'Real Realism' of John Cassavetes." *Film Quarterly* 52, no. 3 (1999): 2–16.

Berlingske Tidende. "Generaldirektøren og den evige fred: Filmens forkyndelse af tanken om Europas forenede stater" [The Director General and Eternal Peace: Film and the Idea of the United States of Europe]. July 14, 1917. Danish Film Institute archive, Copenhagen.

Bordwell, David. "A Strong Sense of Narrative Desire: A Decade of Danish Film." *FILM* (Magazine of the Danish Film Institute), no. 34 (2004): 24–27.

Boym, Svetlana. *The Future of Nostalgia*. New York: Basic Books, 2001.

———. "Nostalgic Technology: Notes for an Off-Modern Manifesto." *Svetlana Boym | Media Art*, n.d. http://www.svetlanaboym.com/manifesto.htm. Accessed March 27, 2012.

———. "The Off-Modern Mirror." *e-flux*, no. 19 (2010). http://www.e-flux.com/journal/the-off-modern-mirror.

Bruno, Giuliana. *Atlas of Emotion: Journeys in Art, Architecture, and Film*. London: Verso, 2002.

B.T. "*Festen* er forbi på Broadway" [*The Celebration* Is Over on Broadway]. May 17, 2006. Danish Film Institute archive, Copenhagen.

Cassavetes, John. *Cassavetes on Cassavetes*. Edited by Raymond Carney. London: Faber and Faber, 2001.

Christensen, Claus. "The Celebration of Rules." *P.O.V.*, no. 10 (2000). http://pov.imv.au.dk/Issue_10/section_3/artc3A.html.

———. "Der var engang en fest" [Once Upon a Time There Was a Party]. *Filmmagasinet Ekko*, no. 18 (2003). http://www.ekkofilm.dk/essays.asp?table=essays&id=19.

———. "Festen der forsvandt" [The Party That Disappeared]. *Weekendavisen*, May 4, 2000. http://www.weekendavisen.dk/.

———. "It's All about Taking Chances: An Interview with Thomas Vinterberg." *FILM* (Magazine of the Danish Film Institute), no. 22 (2002): 3–4.

———. "Reklamefilm åbnede *Festen*" [Advertisement Got *The Celebration* Started]. *Filmmagasinet Ekko*, August 28, 2003. http://www.ekkofilm.dk/?allowbreak=false&id=28.

———. "Stadig tvivl om *Festen*" [There's Still Doubt about *The Celebration*]. *Weekendavisen*, June 22, 2000. http://www.weekendavisen.dk/.

Connerton, Paul. *How Societies Remember*. Cambridge: Cambridge University Press, 1989.

Conrich, Ian, and Estella Tincknell. "Film Purity, the Neo-Bazinian Ideal, and Humanism in Dogma 95." *P.O.V.*, no. 10 (2000). http://pov.imv.au.dk/Issue_10/section_4/artc7A.html.

Danish Film Institute. "Vinterberg til Cannes Festival" [Vinterberg to Cannes Festival]. April 19, 2012. http://www.dfi.dk/Nyheder/NyhederFraDFI/2012/Vinterberg-til-Cannes-Festival.aspx.

Dean, Tacita. *FILM: Tacita Dean*. Edited by Nicholas Cullinan. Unilever Series. London: Tate Publishing, 2011.

———. "Save Celluloid, for Art's Sake." *Guardian*, February 22, 2011. http://www.guardian.co.uk/artanddesign/2011/feb/22/tacita-dean-16mm-film.

Deleuze, Gilles. *Cinema 1: The Movement-Image*. Translated by Hugh Tomlinson and Barbara Habberjam. London: Continuum, 1986.

Dinesen, Isak. "The Blank Page." In *Last Tales*, 99–105. New York: Random House, 1957.

Dixon, Wheeler Winston. *The Films of Jean-Luc Godard*. Albany: State University of New York Press, 1997.

Dogme95, Official Website. Archived by the Internet Archive at http://web.archive.org/web/20080420163820/www.dogme95.dk/menu/menuset.htm. Accessed February 14, 2011.

Eakin, Emily. "Celluloid Hero." *New Yorker*, October 31, 2011, 54.

Ehrenstein, David. "Film in the Age of Video: 'Oh, We Don't Know Where

We're Going but We're on Our Way.'" *Film Quarterly* 49, no. 3 (1996): 38–42.

Eldridge, David. *Festen* [The Celebration]. Modern Plays. London: Methuen Drama, 2004.

Elsaesser, Thomas, ed. *Harun Farocki: Working on the Sight-Lines*. Amsterdam: Amsterdam University Press, 2004.

Fonsmark, Anne-Birgitte, ed. *Hammershøi > Dreyer: The Magic of Images*. Copenhagen: Ordrupgaard Museum, 2006.

Foucault, Michel. "Different Spaces." In *Essential Works of Foucault, 1954–1984*. Vol. 2, *Aesthetics, Method, and Epistemology*, edited by James D. Faubion, translated by Robert Hurley et al., 175–86. London: Penguin, 1998.

French, Philip. "Spin Cycle: The Perils of Political Intrigue Are Examined in a Powerful Danish Thriller." *Observer*, September 25, 2005. http://www.guardian.co.uk/theobserver/2005/sep/25/features.review47.

Gade, Rune, and Anne Jerslev, eds. *Performative Realism: Interdisciplinary Studies in Art and Media*. Copenhagen: Museum Tusculanum Press, 2005.

Gasværket Teater. "Pressemeddelelse: Thomas Vinterbergs *Festen*" [Press Release: Thomas Vinterberg's *The Celebration*]. October 2007. http://www.gasvaerket.dk/.

Gaut, Berys. "Naked Film: Dogma and Its Limits." In *Purity and Provocation: Dogma 95*, edited by Mette Hjort and Scott MacKenzie, 89–100. London: British Film Institute, 2003.

Green Jensen, Bo. "Interview: Premiere; Manden, der gik baglæns" [Interview: Premiere; The Man Who Walked Backwards]. (Includes an interview with Thomas Vinterberg.) *Weekendavisen*, March 26, 2010. http://www.weekendavisen.dk/.

———. "Redux: En lille film om nåde" [Redux: A Little Film about Grace]. *Weekendavisen*, March 26, 2010. http://www.weekendavisen.dk/.

Gunning, Tom. "Now You See It, Now You Don't: The Temporality of the Cinema of Attractions." In *The Silent Cinema Reader*, edited by Lee Grieveson and Peter Krämer, 41–50. London: Routledge, 2004.

Haraway, Donna. *When Species Meet*. Minneapolis: University of Minnesota Press, 2008.

Harrison, Rebecca. "Haunted Screens and Spiritual Scenes: Film as a Medium in the Cinema of Carl Theodor Dreyer." *Scandinavica* 48, no. 1 (2009): 32–43.

Hemming, Sarah. Review of *Festen*, adapted by David Eldridge, directed by Rufus Norris, Almeida Theatre, London. *Financial Times*, March 29, 2004, London edition 1, Arts section, 17.

Hjort, Mette. *Lone Scherfig's "Italian for Beginners."* Nordic Film Classics. Seattle: University of Washington Press; Copenhagen: Museum Tusculanum Press, 2010.

———. *Small Nation, Global Cinema: The New Danish Cinema*. Minneapolis: University of Minnesota Press, 2005.

Hjort, Mette, and Ib Bondebjerg, eds. *The Danish Directors: Dialogues on a Contemporary National Cinema*. Bristol, U.K.: Intellect Books, 2000.

Hjort, Mette, and Scott MacKenzie. Introduction to *Purity and Provocation: Dogma 95*, edited by Mette Hjort and Scott MacKenzie, 1–30. London: British Film Institute, 2003.

Information. "Ti år med Koplevs Krydsfelt" [Ten Years with *Koplev's Crossword*]. December 30, 2003. http://www.information.dk/89119.

Jerslev, Anne. "Dogma 95, Lars von Trier's *The Idiots*, and the 'Idiot Project.'" In *Realism and "Reality" in Film and Media*, edited by Anne Jerslev, 41–65. Copenhagen: Museum Tusculanum Press, 2002.

Jessen, Lisbeth. "All You Need Is Love, God, Power or Money—an Essay on Radio Documentaries." *International Feature Conference*. June 8, 2004. http://ifc.blog-city.com/essay_on_documentaries__lisbeth_jessen.htm.

———. *Efter "Festen"* [After *The Celebration*]. Radio montage. Danmarks Radio, P1. First broadcast September 27, 2003, 16.00. http://www.dr.dk/P1/Dokumentarzonen/Udsendelser/Montage/2003/10/10/000030.htm.

———. "Interview: Lisbeth Jessen." By Birgitte Hornhaver. *Dokumentar-*

zonen [Documentary Zone]. Broadcast August 28, 2007, 14:00, Danmarks Radio P1.

Jones, Rebecca Manson, and Sarah Dickenson. *Festen: Projects Pack*. London: Almeida Projects, 2006. http://www.almeida.co.uk/Downloads/development/resources/FestenTourProjectsPack.pdf.

Kelly, Richard. *The Name of This Book Is Dogme95*. London: Faber and Faber, 2000.

Kennedy, Barbara M. *Deleuze and Cinema: The Aesthetics of Sensation*. Edinburgh: Edinburgh University Press, 2000.

Knudsen, Britta Timm, and Bodil Marie Thomsen. Introduction to *Virkelighedshunger: Nyrealismen i visuel optik* [Reality-Hunger: New Realism in Visual Optics], edited by Britta Timm Knudsen and Bodil Marie Thomsen, 7–27. Copenhagen: Tiderne Skifter, 2002.

———, eds. *Virkelighedshunger: Nyrealismen i visuel optik* [Reality-Hunger: New Realism in a Visual Perspective]. Copenhagen: Tiderne Skifter, 2002.

Kolstrup, Søren. "The Press and DOGMA 95." *P.O.V.*, no. 10 (2000). http://pov.imv.au.dk/Issue_10/section_4/artc3A.html.

Koplev, Kjeld. "Læserbreve: Koplevs køkken" [Readers' Letters: Koplev's Kitchen]. *Information*, August 16, 2006. http://www.information.dk/127934.

Koutsourakis, Angelos. "John Cassavetes: The First Dogme Director?" *Bright Lights Film Journal*, no. 63 (2009). http://www.brightlightsfilm.com/63/63cassavetes.php.

Kouvaros, George. "Where Does It Happen? The Place of Performance in the Work of John Cassavetes." *Screen* 39, no. 3 (1998): 244–58.

Larsen, Rune Engelbreth. "Støtteerklæring til Zentropas Dannebroginitiativ" [Declaration of Support for Zentropa's Danish Flag Initiative]. Humanisme.dk, June 5, 2004. http://www.humanisme.dk/debat/debat134.php.

Lauridsen, Palle Schantz. "*The Celebration*: Classical Drama and Docu Soap Style." *P.O.V.*, no. 10 (2000). http://pov.imv.au.dk/Issue_10/section_3/artc1A.html.

Lehrer, Jeremy. "Denmark's DV Director Thomas Vinterberg Delves into *The Celebration*." (Includes an interview with Thomas Vinterberg.) *indieWIRE*, October 14, 1998. http://www.indiewire.com/article/denmarks_dv_director_thomas_vinterberg_delves_into_the_celebration.

Manovich, Lev. *The Language of New Media*. Cambridge, Mass.: MIT Press, 2001.

Margolies, Eleanor. "Vagueness Gridlocked: A Map of the Smells of New York." In *The Smell Culture Reader*, edited by Jim Drobnick, 107–17. Oxford, U.K.: Berg, 2005.

Marks, Laura U. "How Electrons Remember." In *Touch: Sensuous Theory and Multisensory Media*, 161–76. Minneapolis: University of Minnesota Press, 2002.

———. "Loving a Disappearing Image." *Cinémas: Revue d études cinématographiques / Cinémas: Journal of Film Studies* 8, nos. 1–2 (1997): 93–111.

———. "Loving a Disappearing Image." In *Touch: Sensuous Theory and Multisensory Media*, 91–110. Minneapolis: University of Minnesota Press, 2002.

———. *The Skin of the Film: Intercultural Cinema, Embodiment, and the Senses*. Durham, N.C.: Duke University Press, 2000.

———. "Thinking Multisensory Culture." *Paragraph* 31, no. 2 (2008): 123–37.

———. *Touch: Sensuous Theory and Multisensory Media*. Minneapolis: University of Minnesota Press, 2002.

Massumi, Brian. *Parables for the Virtual: Movement, Affect, Sensation*. Durham, N.C.: Duke University Press, 2002.

Matthews, Peter. Review of *Festen*, directed by Thomas Vinterberg. *Sight and Sound*, March 1999. http://old.bfi.org.uk/sightandsound/review/49.

Meigh-Andrews, Chris. *A History of Video Art: The Development of Form and Function*. Oxford, U.K.: Berg, 2006.

Monaco, James. *The Dictionary of New Media: The New Digital World* of *Video, Audio, and Print*. New York: Harbor Electronic Publishers, 2007.

———. *How to Read a Film: Movies, Media, and Beyond*. Oxford: Oxford University Press, 2009.

Monahan, Mark. "Film-Makers on Film: Thomas Vinterberg; Thomas Vinterberg Talks to Mark Monahan about Andrei Tarkovsky's *Stalker* (1979)." *Telegraph*, February 16, 2004. http://www.telegraph.co.uk/culture/film/3612441/Film-makers-on-film-Thomas-Vinterberg.html.

Mørch, Søren. *Den sidste Danmarkshistorie* [The Last History of Denmark]. Copenhagen: Gad, 1996.

Mortensen, Tina Gylling, Claus Flygare, and Thomas Bendixen. "Debat: Åbent brev fra Mammutteatret" [Debate: Open Letter from Mammoth Theatre Company]. *Information*, August 18, 2006, 32–33.

Mulvey, Laura. *Death 24x a Second: Stillness and the Moving Image*. London: Reaktion Books, 2006.

Nagib, Lúcia, and Cecília Mello, eds. *Realism and the Audiovisual Media*. Basingstoke: Palgrave Macmillan, 2009.

Politiken. "Afgangsfilm var den bedste" [Graduation Film Was the Best]. February 21, 1994. Danish Film Institute archive, Copenhagen.

Prince, Stephen. "True Lies: Perceptual Realism, Digital Images, and Film Theory." *Film Quarterly* 49, no. 3 (1996): 27–37.

Rees, A. L. *A History of Experimental Film and Video*. London: British Film Institute, 1999.

Rees, Ellen. "In My Father's House Are Many Mansions: Transgressive Space in Three Dogma 95 Films." *Scandinavica* 43, no. 2 (2004): 165–82.

Rodowick, David. *The Virtual Life of Film*. Cambridge, Mass.: Harvard University Press, 2007.

Rugg, Linda Haverty. "Globalization and the Auteur: Ingmar Bergman Projected Internationally." In *Transnational Cinema in a Global North: Nordic Cinema in Transition*, edited by Andrew Nestingen and Trevor Elkington, 221–59. Detroit: Wayne State University Press, 2005.

Rukov, Mogens. "Adventures of a Productive Idiot." *Guardian*, October 26, 2002, Saturday section, 17.

———. "Det smukkeste er hengivelsen: Interview med Mogens Rukov" [The Most Beautiful Thing Is Surrender: Interview with Mogens Rukov]. By Nikolaj Mangurten Lassen. *Weekendavisen*, September 9, 2010. http://www.weekendavisen.dk/.

Sandbye, Mette, ed. *Virkelighed! Virkelighed! Avantgardens realisme* [Reality! Reality! The Realism of the Avant-Garde]. Copenhagen: Tiderne Skifter, 2003.

Schepelern, Peter. *Danish Film History*. http://www.dfi.dk/English/Danish-Film-History.aspx.

———. "Film according to Dogma: Ground Rules, Obstacles, and Liberations." In *Transnational Cinema in a Global North: Nordic Cinema in Transition*, edited by Andrew Nestingen and Trevor Elkington, 73–107. Detroit: Wayne State University Press, 2005.

———. "Film ifølge Dogme: Spilleregler, forhindringer og befrielser" [Film according to Dogma: Ground Rules, Obstacles, and Liberations]. In *Nationale spejlinger: Tendenser in ny dansk film* [National Reflections: Tendencies in New Danish Film], edited by Anders Toftgaard and Ian Halvdan Hawkesworth, 61–108. Copenhagen: Museum Tusculanum Press, 2003.

Searle, Adrian. "Tacita Dean: *Film*—Review." *Guardian*, October 10, 2011. http://www.guardian.co.uk/artanddesign/2011/oct/10/tacita-dean-film-review.

Shaviro, Steven. *Post-Cinematic Affect*. Winchester, U.K.: Zero Books, 2010.

Sierz, Alex. "In Britain, the Writer Is King." *Financial Times*, March 17, 2004, London edition, 15.

Simons, Jan. "Playing the Waves: The Name of the Game Is Dogme95." In *Cinephilia: Movies, Love, and Memory*, edited by Marijke de Valck and Malte Hagener, 181–96. Amsterdam: Amsterdam University Press, 2005.

Skyum-Nielsen, Erik. *Engle i sneen: Lyrik og prosa i 90erne* [Angels in the

Snow: Poetry and Prose in the 1990s]. Copenhagen: Gyldendal, 2000.

Spielmann, Yvonne. *Video: The Reflexive Medium*. Translated by Anja Welle and Stan Jones. Cambridge, Mass.: MIT Press, 2008.

Stevenson, Jack. *Dogme Uncut: Lars von Trier, Thomas Vinterberg, and the Gang That Took on Hollywood*. Santa Monica, Calif.: Santa Monica Press, 2003.

Strauven, Wanda, ed. *The Cinema of Attractions Reloaded*. Amsterdam: Amsterdam University Press, 2006.

Tarkovsky, Andrei. *Sculpting in Time: Reflections on the Cinema*. Translated by Kitty Hunter-Blair. Austin: University of Texas Press, 2005.

Thobo-Carlsen, Jesper. "*Festen* udeblev på Broadway" [*The Celebration* Out of It on Broadway]. *Berlingske Tidende*, April 12, 2006. Clippings folder, Danish Film Institute archive, Copenhagen.

Thomsen, Bodil Marie. "Lear—liar—real: Om Jean-Luc Godards *King Lear* og Kristian Levrings *The King Is Alive*" [Lear—Liar—Real: On Jean-Luc Godard's *King Lear* and Kristian Levring's *The King Is Alive*]. In *Om som om: Antologi om realisme* [On "As If": An Anthology about Realism], edited by Stefan Iversen, Heidi Jørgensen, and Henrik Skov Nielsen, 148–67. Nørhaven, Viborg: Akademisk Forlag, 2002.

———. "Sansernes realisme—om etik, rum og begivenhed i Lars von Triers 90'er-trilogi" [Realism of the Senses—on Ethics, Space, and Event in Lars von Trier's 1990s Trilogy]. In *Virkelighedshunger: Nyrealismen i visuel optik* [Reality-Hunger: New Realism in Visual Optics], edited by Britta Timm Knudsen and Bodil Marie Thomsen, 111–39. Copenhagen, Tiderne Skifter, 2002.

Thomson, C. Claire. "Air, Scent, and the Senses: Unni Straume's *Derailment*." *Short Film Studies* 1, no. 2 (2011): 245–49.

———. "Cultivate the Nation, Don't Nationalise Culture! Intercultural Cinema in a Small Language Department." Liaison Magazine (*LLAS Subject Centre*), no. 4 (2010). http://www.llas.ac.uk/resourcedownloads/179/liaison_jan10.pdf.

———. "It's All about Snow: Limning the Posthuman Body in *Солярис/ Solaris* (Tarkovsky, 1972) and *It's All about Love* (Vinterberg,

2003)." *New Cinemas: Journal of Contemporary Film* 5, no. 1 (2007): 3–21.

Trier, Lars von. "Project 'Open Film Town.'" In *The Danish Directors: Dialogues on a Contemporary National Cinema*, edited by Mette Hjort and Ib Bondebjerg, 224–27. Bristol, U.K.: Intellect Books, 2000.

———. *Trier on von Trier*. Edited by Stig Björkman. Translated by Neil Smith. London: Faber and Faber, 2003.

Usai, Paolo Cherchi. *The Death of Cinema: History, Cultural Memory, and the Digital Dark Age*. London: British Film Institute, 2001.

Vinterberg, Thomas. "Celebrating Limitations: An Interview with Thomas Vinterberg." By Bo Green Jensen. *Weekendavisen*, April 1998. Archived at http://web.archive.org/web/20070708192051/www.dogme95.dk/celebration/index.htm.

———. *Festen*. Copenhagen: Per Kofoed, 1998.

———. Interview by Anne Mette Traberg Jørgensen. Copenhagen, August 2007. Unpublished. Danish transcript in the author's possession.

Vinterberg, Thomas, and Mogens Rukov. *Festen: Fête de famille* [Festen: The Family Party]. Adapted from the film by Bo hr. Hansen. Translated from the Danish into French by Daniel Benoin. With the collaboration of Sejer Andersen. Arles: Actes Sud, 2003.

———. "Mere end én gang tænkte vi på Hamlet" [More than Once We Thought of Hamlet]. In *Festen og andre skandaler: Udvalgte artikler 1992–2002* [*The Celebration* and Other Scandals: Selected Writings, 1992–2002]. By Mogens Rukov, edited by Claus Christensen, 75–80. Copenhagen: Lindhardt and Ringhof, 2002.

Index

16mm: and *Festen*, 118; film format, 60, 75, 120; processing of, 60–61; and *Submarino*, 48, 177. See also 35mm; celluloid; Dean, Tacita; film grain; indexicality; intermediality

35mm: and art, 62; and distribution, 58–59; and Dogma 95 rules, 28, 57–60, 61, 69, 188n25; and *Festen*, 118, 160–61, 167; film format, 67, 75, 120, 153; and nostalgia, 69. See also 16mm; celluloid; Dean, Tacita; film grain; indexicality; intermediality

acting, 34, 81, 149
affect, 7, 9–10, 11, 31–32, 34–35, 36, 82, 84–87, 90, 109–16, 117, 122
affection-image, 82
affective contract, 11, 31–32, 82, 90
Allan, 127–38

Almeida Theatre (London), 140, 144, 196n4
A Man Comes Home (Vinterberg), 48, 176
analogue technologies, 6, 54–56, 152–53, 189n35; and indexicality, 31, 56, 59, 62, 63–69, 121, 158; and intermedial transfer, 118–23; and nostalgia, 60–63, 67–69
Andersen, Hans Christian, 19
Angelic Conversation, The (Jarman), 120
architecture: and camerawork in *Festen*, 97–104; and Danish Cultural Canon, 35; of Skjoldenæsholm hotel, 91, 93–97; of the theater, 141–42, 143; and *The Word* (Dreyer), 156–58, 199n7
Arriflex camera, 75
audience, 49, 79, 130, 133, 146, 148, 149; and acting, 79–82, 141; and Dogma 95 manifesto, 164; extras as, 79

August, Bille, 19
auteur, 11; and Dogma 95, 41–45, 60, 163; Vinterberg as, 46–50
authorship, 44, 135–38
Axel, Gabriel, 19, 115

Babette's Feast (Axel), 19, 115
Barbican (London), 149, 198n28
Barthes, Roland: and authorship, 44; *Camera Lucida*, 65–66, 157
Baudrillard, Jean, 63–64
Bazin, André: "The Ontology of the Photographic Image," 64–66, 157; "Theater and Cinema: Part Two," 139, 140–42, 147–48, 197n8
Bergman, Ingmar, 4, 113, 172; and Dogma 95, 73–74; and French New Wave, 46
Blixen, Karen. *See* Dinesen, Isak
Blom, August, 18
Blur (band), 173–74
Bodil awards, 173
Bolex camera, 75
Bordwell, David, 17
Boym, Svetlana, 51, 59–60, 68. *See also* nostalgia
Boy Who Walked Backwards, The (Vinterberg), 46, 49, 172
Breaking the Waves (von Trier), 20, 75
Broadway (New York), 8, 140, 144, 148, 179n3
Bruno, Giuliana: *Atlas of Emotion*, 91, 95–97, 104, 108–10, 118, 192n29, 193n7
budget, 74, 77; and Dogma 95, 57–59

Cage, Nicolas, 4
Cannes film festival, 19, 37–38, 49, 143, 173, 177
canted angle, 97–99, 108
"cartoon crisis," 32
Cassavetes, John, 78–85, 88–90, 191n9
celluloid: in art, 62; and *Festen*, 75; threat to, 61, 68; transfer to, 120–21; Lars von Trier and, 120. *See also* 16mm; 35mm; Dean, Tacita; film grain; indexicality; intermediality
centenary of cinema, 3, 38, 53–54, 59
Christensen, Benjamin, 18
Christensen, Charlotte Bruus, 177
Christensen, Claus, 130–31, 135–36, 196n19
Christian (character), 12–14, 27–28, 33, 34, 73–74, 78–79, 85, 87, 88, 98–104, 105–06, 109–17, 160; and Allan, 127–28, 130, 133–38; and close-ups, 81–82; and dream sequence, 154–55; and stage versions, 143–49
cinema of attractions, 39, 184n3
cinematography: and Dogma 95 constraints, 27; in *Festen*, 68, 74–77, 119–23, 152; in *It's All about Love*, 175; Vinterberg and, 82; *See also* Mantle, Anthony Dod
cinéma vérité, 74, 75
cinephilia, 19–20
class. *See* social class
close-up, 78–82, 87, 88, 90, 101–02, 115, 149

computer-generated imagery (CGI), 39, 56, 67, 68–69. See also digital video; new media; special effects
conservation, of film, 53, 68–69
constraints, 6, 36, 118
Copenhagen, 21, 26, 33, 40, 49, 93, 106, 128, 131, 163, 166, 168, 174, 177

Dancer in the Dark (von Trier), 177
Danish cinema: Danish language in, 18, 19, 49, 177; golden age of, 17–18, 39; history of, 18–20
Danish Cultural Canon, 6, 35, 160–61
Danish Film Institute, x, 20–21, 49, 159
Danmarks Radio, 21, 58, 132, 167, 179n4
D-Day, 174
Dean, Tacita, 60–62
Dear Wendy (Vinterberg), 48, 175
death of film, 11, 51–54, 59, 60–62, 66–67, 122
Deleuze, Gilles, 82
Denmark: architectural history of, 93–94; cinema history of, 17–24, 136; language norms, 18, 19, 32–33; literature of, 29–32; nationalism in, 32–36; radio in, 129; reception of *Festen* in, 8, 142, 173; social norms, 32–36, 79
digital video: cameras, 40, 65–67; and cinema history, 5–6; DVD format, 53–55, 151–53; and editing, 54–5. See also new media

Dinesen, Isak, 194n7
direct cinema, 75, 79, 84
distribution, 4, 28, 43, 53–55, 58–59, 61, 159
Dogma 95: and digital technology, 39, 66–67; international impact of, 37–38; launch of, 3–4; manifesto, 3–9, 11, 38–45, 46, 50, 51, 53, 59, 63, 66, 68–69, 153, 163–64; vow of chastity (rules), 3–5, 20–21, 25–31, 36, 40–44, 47, 57–60, 83–84, 89, 91–93, 106, 109, 118, 122–23, 138, 165–66
Dreyer, Carl Theodor, 19, 120, 156–60, 199n7
Dyrholm, Trine, 169, 173. See also Pia (character)

editing: and analogue video, 120; and digital technology, 54–55, 59, 62, 187n7; in *Festen*, 97, 104–07, 117, 147, 184–85n8
Eisenstein, Sergei, 95, 193n7
Eldridge, David, 140, 144–48, 153
Element of Crime, The (von Trier), 19
Elfelt, Peter, 17
Else (character), 13–14, 33–34, 73, 103, 115, 117, 128, 145, 168
ethnicity, 32–36
event: and analogue technology, 11, 52, 63–64, 152–53; and digital technology, 52, 65–66; and handheld camera, 80–88, 104; and realism, 29–32, 36; and sound, 116–17, 121

INDEX 215

Faces (Cassavetes), 77–82
Fanny and Alexander (Bergman), 172, 194n8
Farocki, Harun, 76, 190n4
Filmbyen, 21–22
film grain, 110, 117–23
Filmhouse, The (Edinburgh), 7
film language, 40, 110, 118–19, 142
Film Town. *See* Filmbyen
financing, 4, 19–21, 25, 57–59, 167, 177
formal breakthrough (Danish literature), 30–32
Foucault, Michel, 94, 192n4
French (language), 51–52, 197n12
French New Wave, 11, 40–41, 46, 51–52, 75, 163
French, Philip, 17
funding. *See* financing
Funeral, The (Vinterberg and Rukov), 149–50

Gbatokai (character), 13, 32–36, 85, 109, 145, 153, 169, 184n35
genre, 3, 17, 24, 28, 47, 88–89, 165, 175
globalization, 4, 32, 38, 50
Godard, Jean-Luc, 41, 51–53, 75–76, 185n9, 190n3
Greatest Heroes, The (Vinterberg), 46, 77, 173
Greenaway, Peter, 120
Hammershøi, Vilhelm, 154, 199n7
handheld camera, 7, 11, 26, 28, 58, 73–90, 91, 98, 115–16
Hansen, Bo hr., 142–45, 149, 172, 173, 197n10, 197n12, 197n13
haptic, the, 11, 106, 108–23

216 INDEX

Helene (character), 12–14, 32–33, 79, 85, 87, 88, 98–99, 102–06, 109–115, 121, 143–47, 154, 160–61, 168, 184n8
Helge (character), 12–14, 33, 73, 78–79, 81, 88, 95, 98, 101–04, 115–17, 121, 127–30, 143–46, 149–50, 160, 168, 196n19
Helmut (character), 12, 33, 74, 103, 113, 128, 145, 154
heterotopia, 94–95, 192n4
Hilden, Jytte, 20–21
Histoire(s) du cinéma (Godard), 51–52
historiography, 30–32
Hitchcock, Alfred, 43
Hjort, Mette, ix, 8, 17–20, 29, 38, 44, 196n19
Holger-Madsen, 18
Hollywood, 67, 139
Hunt, The (Vinterberg), 49, 177

Idiots, The (von Trier), 31–32, 37, 79, 191n14
improvisation, 40, 79–80, 82–86, 192n30
incest, 27, 117, 129–32, 136, 153. *See also* sexual abuse
indexicality, 11, 30–31, 39–40, 56–60, 62–69, 121, 140–41, 152, 158–59, 161
intellectual property, 134–37
interface, 62, 68
intermediality, 8, 48, 54, 58, 118–23, 135–36
irony, 25, 41–44, 50
Italian for Beginners (Scherfig), 44

It's All About Love (Vinterberg), 46–48, 174–75, 186n22

Jarman, Derek, 120
Jensen, Peter Aalbæk, 21
Jessen, Lisbeth, 131–37

Kim (character), 13, 127, 146, 169
Klingenfeldt-Hansen family. *See* individual characters' first names
Koplev, Kjeld, 129–34, 135–37
Koplevs krydsfelt (radio program), 129–34
kortprosa (literary genre), 30
Kragh-Jacobsen, Søren, 21, 42, 174
Kulturkanon. *See* Danish Cultural Canon

language. *See under* film language; Denmark: language norms
Lars (character), 89, 98–99, 102, 111–12, 145–48
Larsen, Thomas Bo, 86, 168, 172, 173, 176. *See also* Michael (character)
Last Round (Vinterberg), 46, 172
Levring, Kristian, 21, 42, 174, 185n9
light, 64–66, 91
lighting, 27, 85, 98–103, 111, 118–23, 154–57, 165, 176
Linda (character), 12, 73, 105, 108, 111, 128, 143–48, 153–55, 158–61, 169
London Film Festival, 49
Lumière brothers, 53
Lyric Theatre (London), 140, 152

MacNeil, Ian, 144
Mantle, Anthony Dod, 27, 28, 57, 68, 76–77, 89–90, 105, 118–23, 152, 168, 175, 177
Manovich, Lev, 39–40, 56, 62, 67, 96, 105, 180n8, 188n24
Marks, Laura U., 66, 110, 116, 118, 121, 151–53, 198n1
Massaci, Vlad, 149
Massumi, Brian, 9–10
Medea (von Trier), 120
media, 5, 8, 10, 11, 43, 128–38, 140, 151–53. *See also* intermediality; new media; press, the
Metallica, 176
Mette (character), 12, 85–87, 89, 98, 145–47, 169
Michael (character), 12–14, 33–34, 85–88, 89, 97–105, 115, 121, 130, 145–47, 168
Mikkelsen, Brian, 35, 148
Mikkelsen, Mads, 177
Moritzen, Henning, 78–79, 168. *See also* Helge (character)
Mulvey, Laura, 52–55, 66, 159, 161
music, 26, 101, 144, 165, 168, 176

narrative: and affect, 9–10, 81–82; and the close-up, 82–83; and Dogma 95, 5, 26, 30–31, 39–40, 93, 106; in *Festen* (film) 44–45, 111–12, 134–38, 143, 154, 158; in *Festen* (stage plays), 142–48; and film history, 5, 7, 17, 159–61; historical, 10–11; in *It's All About Love*, 47–48; master (grand) narratives, 10, 29–31; and new media, 159–61

national allegory, 32–36
National Film School of Denmark, 19–20, 23–24, 77, 172
nationalism, 32–36
Natsværmerpris, 46
new media, 6–7, 151–53, 159–61, 180n8, 189n35; Dogma 95 and, 21–23, 31–32, 39, 53–69, 199n11; realism and 31–32; Lars von Trier and, 21–23; Thomas Vinterberg and, 66–68, 118. See also computer-generated imagery; digital video; special effects
Nielsen, Asta, 18
Nimbus Film, 130, 167
non-place, 95
Nordic Council Film Prize, 48, 177
Norris, Rufus, 144–48
nostalgia, 51, 59–69
Nottara Theater (Bucharest), 149
nouvelle vague. See French New Wave

Olsen, Ole, 18
Ordet. See Word, The (Dreyer)
Óskarsdóttir, Valdís, 45, 54, 168

painting, 48, 62, 64, 96, 101–02, 105, 154, 199n7
Pelle the Conqueror (August), 19
Pia (character), 13–14, 87–88, 105, 109, 111, 113, 115, 145, 146–48, 153–55, 169
plot: and Dogma 95, 27–28, 31–32, 109, 164; of Festen (film), 27, 95, 109, 135–37; of Festen (stage plays), 142–8. See also narrative

press, the: Dogma 95 and, 179n2; Thomas Vinterberg and, 46–50
props: and Dogma 95, 3, 25–26, 106, 109, 165; in Festen (film), 11, 91–92, 106–117, 122
Prospero's Books (Greenaway), 120

racism, 32–35
radio, 5, 12, 28, 128–37,
realism, 11, 29–32, 34, 36, 65, 74, 88, 146, 172, 183n27, 191n14. See also Cassavetes; reality
reality, 11, 31, 39, 44, 56. See also realism
Ringsted, 26, 93. See also Skjoldenæsholm
Robert award, 173, 175
Rubin, Marla, 144–45
Rukov, Mogens, 24, 37–38, 44–45, 54–55, 127, 129, 136–38, 142–45, 149–50, 153, 168, 173, 174, 176, 196n17, 197n12

Schepelern, Peter, ix, 21, 83, 133, 181n5, 197n10, 197n13
script-writing, 5, 21, 23–24, 44–45, 129, 142, 153. See also narrative; plot
sense memory, 11, 31–32, 69, 108–17, 118, 122–23; food and, 115–16; smell and, 108–09, 110, 115–16, 194n12; sound and, 116–17. See also haptic, the
sexual abuse, 13–14, 27, 73, 78–79, 117, 129–30, 132, 148, 153, 160. See also incest

Skjoldenæsholm (hotel and conference centre), 26, 91–107, 111, 167, 192n2
Slaget på tasken (Vinterberg), 171
Snowblind (Vinterberg), 171
social class, 32–33, 176
sound: and Dogma 95, 26, 165; in *Festen* (film), 12, 26, 28, 82, 102, 116–17, 121, 122, 154–55, 160, 168; in *Festen* (stage plays), 145, 148; in film, 18. *See also* music; sense memory
special effects, 3, 39, 175. *See also* computer-generated imagery; digital video; new media
spectacle, 39, 64
Stalker (Tarkovsky), 82
state support, 19–21
Steadicam, 74–76
Steen, Paprika, 79, 168, 173, 184n8, 191n9. *See also* Helene (character)
story. *See* narrative; plot
style: and Danish film industry, 24; and Dogma 95, 9, 41, 74; and French New Wave, 41; in *Festen* (film), 5–6, 74; in *Festen* (stage plays), 12, 146–48; of Thomas Vinterberg, 9, 77–78, 88–90. *See also* auteur; authorship; Vinterberg, Thomas
Submarino (Vinterberg), 48–49, 177

supernatural, the, 11–12, 153

tapestry, 105–06
Tarkovsky, Andrei, 82, 186n22
Tate Modern, 60–61
texture, 7, 9, 69, 106, 110, 114, 115, 121, 122–23, 128, 160–61. *See also* haptic, the
Thomsen, Ulrich, 133, 168, 171, 173, 196n19. *See also* Christian (character)

utopia, 51, 60

Vertov, Dziga, 76
Vinterberg, Thomas: as auteur, 11, 37–38, 46–50; cameo role, 43; career, 7–8, 46–50, 149–50. *See also* individual film titles
violence, 27, 48, 117, 121, 175. *See also* incest; sexual abuse
Visconti, Luchino, 113
von Sachs, Helmut. *See* Helmut (character)
von Trier, Lars, 3, 17, 19, 20, 21, 25, 29, 31, 35, 36, 37, 38, 41, 42, 48, 49, 75, 78, 79, 89, 120, 130, 174, 175, 177

West End (London), 139
Word, The (Dreyer), 156–60

Zentropa, 21–23, 182n17, 184n36

INDEX 219